VERNON LEE

VERNON LEE

Sondeep Kandola

NORTHCOTE
BRITISH
COUNCIL

First published in 2010 by Northcote House Publishers Ltd, Horndon, Tavistock, Devon, PL19 9NQ, United Kingdom.
Tel: +44 (0) 1822 810066 Fax: +44 (0) 1822 810034.

British Library Cataloguing-in-Publication Data
A catalogue record for this book is available from the British Library

ISBN 978-0-7463-1171-4 hardcover
ISBN 978-0-7463-1176-9 paperback

Typeset by PDQ Typesetting, Newcastle-under-Lyme
Printed and bound in the United Kingdom

For my beloved grandmother, Joginder Kaur, with love.

Contents

Acknowledgements

My thanks, as ever, to Isobel Armstrong for her encouragement during the conception and writing of this book. I am very grateful indeed to Juliette Taylor-Batty and Ana Parejo-Vadillo for their insightful comments on individual chapters of this book. I would also like to express my gratitude to Margaret D. Stetz for permitting me to read her essay on 'Prince Alberic and the Snake Lady' prior to its publication. Likewise, I am also grateful to Northcote House for encouragement and helpful suggestions for improving this book. My thanks to Catherine Spooner, John Holmes and Lucy Bending for allowing me to develop my ideas on Lee's experiments in psychological aesthetics at the 'Victorian Modernities' conference organized by the School of English and American Literature at the University of Reading in May 2004. My thanks too to the British Academy for its provision of an Overseas Conference Grant which allowed me to deliver a paper on Vernon Lee, Charlotte Perkins Gilman and Olive Schreiner at the Twenty-First British Women Writers' Conference held at Lafayette, Louisiana in 2005. Part of Chapter One was originally published in 'Vernon Lee: New Woman?', *Women's Writing*, Vol. 12, no. 3, (2005). Thanks to the Taylor & Francis Group for permission to reproduce this material. I am also indebted to Patricia Burdick, the Librarian of Colby College, Maine, USA which holds Lee's copyright, for permission to publish an excerpt from Lee's letters. Finally I should like to thank my parents, Halwinder and Kulwant, for their continued support and encouragement.

Biographical Outline

1856   Violet Paget born 14 October in Boulogne-sur-Mer, France, to Matilda (née Adams) widow of Captain James Lee Hamilton, and Henry Ferguson Paget. The family move periodically between Germany, Switzerland and Italy.

1862   Visits England for the first time.

1870   Publishes her short story 'Les aventures d'une pièce de monnaie' in a Lausanne periodical, *La famille*. Visits her half-brother, Eugene Lee-Hamilton, in Paris.

1873   Family settles in Florence; illness renders Eugene a virtual paraplegic and he returns home.

1875   Adopts pen-name 'Vernon Lee' for a series of articles she publishes in the Italian journal *La Rivista Europea*.

1880   Meets and begins passionate relationship with the poet Mary Robinson. Publishes *Studies of the Eighteenth Century in Italy* and *Tuscan Fairy Tales*.

1881   Publishes *Belcaro: Being Essays on Sundry Aesthetical Questions*. In the course of visiting Mary in London meets, amongst others, Robert Browning, Edmund Gosse, William Morris, Walter Pater and Oscar Wilde.

1882   Visits Pater and his sisters in Oxford.

1883   Publishes *The Prince of the Hundred Soups: A Puppet-Show in Narrative* and *Ottilie: An Eighteenth-Century Idyl*. Guest of Bella Duffy in London.

1884   Publishes *Euphorion: Being Studies of the Antique and the Mediaeval in the Renaissance* and *The Countess of Albany*. Publishes *Miss Brown*. Dedicates it to Henry James. The novel receives poor reviews and offends many members of London's 'high art' circle.

1886   *Baldwin: Being Dialogues on Views and Aspirations* and *A Phantom Lover. A Fantastic Story* published. (*A Phantom*

	Lover republished as 'Oke of Okehurst; Or, The Phantom Lover' in *Hauntings* (1890)).
1887	Meets Clementina (Kit) Anstruther-Thomson. Mary announces surprise engagement to French scholar, James Darmesteter. Lee suffers first attack of neurasthenia. *Juvenilia: Being a Second Series of Essays on Sundry Aesthetical Questions* published.
1888	Despite the Paget family's intervention, Mary marries Darmesteter (August). November: Lee travels to Tangiers and Spain with Evelyn Wimbush to recover her health. Begins 'psychological aesthetics' project with Kit.
1889	The Pagets lease Il Palmerino, Maiano in the hills overlooking Florence.
1890	Publishes *Hauntings: Fantastic Stories.*
1892	Publishes *Vanitas: Polite Stories.* One story of the collection 'Lady Tal' causes a rupture with Henry James.
1893	*Althea: A Second Book of Dialogues on Aspirations and Duties* published. Befriends the composer Ethel Smyth.
1894	Walter Pater (July) and Lee's father, Henry Ferguson Paget (November) die.
1895	*Renaissance Fancies and Studies*, which includes a valedictory to Pater, published.
1896	Mother, Matilda, dies (March). Eugene recovers health and travels to America.
1897	Publishes *Limbo and Other Essays.* Lee and Kit publish the results of their experiments in 'psychological aesthetics' in an article for the *Contemporary Review.* Bernard Berenson, an American scholar of Renaissance art, accuses them of plagiarizing his ideas.
1898	Eugene marries the novelist Annie Holdsworth. Kit leaves Lee to nurse her friend Mrs Christian Head. Kit decides to split her time equally between Lee and Mrs Head.
1899	Publishes *Genius Loci: Notes on Places.*
1900	Mary marries Emile Duclaux. Final split with Kit.
1903	*Ariadne in Mantua* and *Penelope Brandling* published. Birth of her niece Persis.
1904	Befriends H.G. Wells who subsequently manages Lee's publishing affairs. Meets Edith Wharton. Persis dies. Publishes *Pope Jacynth and Other Fantastic Tales* and

	Hortus Vitae: Essays on the Gardening of Life.
1905	*The Enchanted Woods, and Other Essays* published.
1906	Publishes *The Spirit of Rome* and buys Il Palmerino.
1907	Eugene dies (September). Lee travels to Greece and Egypt.
1908	Publishes *The Sentimental Traveller* and *Gospels of Anarchy and Other Contemporary Studies.*
1909	*Laurus Nobilis: Chapters on Art and Life* published.
1912	Publishes *Vital Lies* and *Beauty and Ugliness.*
1913	Publishes *The Beautiful.*
1914	*Louis Norbert: A Two-Fold Romance* and *The Tower of Mirrors* published. The First World War leaves Lee unable to return to Italy after her summer visit to England. Public altercation with Wells over the war. Lee's pacifism proves unpopular and leads to accusations of pro-German sympathies against her.
1915	Publishes *The Ballet of the Nations: a Present-Day Morality.* Joins Ramsay Macdonald's Union of Democratic Control.
1916	Reads *The Ballet* at a UDC meeting.
1920	Publishes *Satan the Waster: A Philosophical War Trilogy.* Returns to Italy.
1921	Kit dies.
1923	Publishes *The Handling of Words and Other Studies in Literary Psychology.*
1924	Publishes and writes an introduction to Kit's pieces of art-criticism, *Art and Man.* University of Durham confers the degree of Doctor of Letters upon Lee.
1925	Publishes *The Golden Keys and Other Essays on the Genius Loci* and *Proteus; or the Future of Intelligence.*
1927	*For Maurice: Five Unlikely Stories* published.
1932	Publishes *Music and Its Lovers: An Empirical Study of Emotional and Imaginative Responses to Music.*
1934	On a visit to England, taken ill and returns to Italy.
1935	Dies at Il Palmerino (13 February) and is buried at the Allori cemetery at Florence.

Abbreviations and References

B	*Belcaro: Being Essays on Sundry Aesthetical Questions* (London: W. Satchell, 1881)
BU	(with C. Anstruther-Thomson) *Beauty and Ugliness and Other Studies in Psychological Aesthetics* (London and New York: John Lane, The Bodley Head, 1912)
BN	*The Ballet of the Nations. A Present–Day Morality* (London: Chatto & Windus, 1915)
E	*Euphorion: Being Studies of the Antique and the Mediaeval in the Renaissance*, 2 vols. (London: T. Fisher Unwin, 1884)
GL	*Genius Loci: Notes on Places* (London: Grant Richards, 1899)
GA	*Gospels of Anarchy and Other Contemporary Studies* (London and Leipzig: T. Fisher Unwin, 1908)
HW	*The Handling of Words* (London: John Lane, The Bodley Head, 1923)
HAOFT	*Hauntings and Other Fantastic Tales*, eds. Catherine Maxwell and Patricia Pulham (Peterborough, Canada: Broadview Press, 2006)
MB	*Miss Brown: A Novel*, 3 vols. (Edinburgh and London: William Blackwood and Sons, 1884)
RFS	*Renaissance Fancies and Studies* (London: Smith, Elder & Co., 1895)
SW	*Satan the Waster. A Philosophic War Trilogy with Notes and Introduction* (London: John Lane, 1920)
V	*Vanitas: Polite Stories* (London: William Heinemann, 1892)
VLL	*Vernon Lee's Letters*, ed. I. Cooper Willis (London: Privately printed, 1937)

Colby   Vineta Colby, *Vernon Lee: A Literary Biography* (Charlottesville and London: University of Virginia Press, 2003)

Gunn   Peter Gunn, *Vernon Lee: Violet Paget, 1856–1935* (London: Oxford University Press, 1964)

Introduction

Over the course of her sixty-year career, Vernon Lee, woman of letters, aesthetician and pacifist, both anticipated, and participated in, the wider shift from Victorian earnestness to Modernist play which shaped British literature at the turn of the twentieth century. English by birth but raised in Europe, Lee was in the unusual position for a Victorian woman of being trained from an early age (as she would later recall) somewhat haphazardly by her mother and her half-brother (the poet Eugene Lee-Hamilton) for a career as a professional writer (see *HW*, 297– 301 and Colby, 6, 12). Critical acclaim came at the early age of twenty-four with the publication of her first book, *Studies of the Eighteenth Century in Italy* (1880), a collection of essays on eighteenth-century opera and comedy from her adopted homeland, which was received as an astoundingly erudite book to have been written by a young woman without any formal education.[1] What followed was a long, prestigious and sometimes controversial career which saw Lee become an uncontested authority on Italian culture, participate, in her fiction and non-fiction writing, in the dominant cultural debates of the day and attempt to sway public opinion internationally on topics such as the First World War and vivisection. It is a testament both to the vitality and continued appeal of Lee's writing that her novels, novellas, supernatural tales, pacifist plays and essays on cultural history and aesthetics have attracted a new generation of readers whose various interests in the Victorian ghost story, the culture of the Victorian *fin de siècle*, precursors to the Modernist movement, literary depictions of non-normative sexualities and European identity have brought them in contact with this pioneering and inventive author.

1

At the age of nineteen, Violet Paget took the masculine *nom de plume* 'Vernon Lee' because, in her own words, she was 'sure that no one reads a woman's writing on art, history or aesthetics with anything but unmitigated contempt' (quoted in Gunn, 66). Where the early careers of the Brontë sisters and novelists George Eliot and George Sand have shown that this strategy was hardly unique, the fact that, despite her gender soon being found out, Lee continued to use her masculine pen-name in public *and* private, is telling. While publicly, her sexual politics were formulated in response, and in reaction, to the permissive and dissident sexual identities propounded in 'high art' circles such as the Pre-Raphaelite Brotherhood and the Aesthetic Movement at the end of the Victorian period, her private emotional life and sexual orientation have proved much more elusive to track. That she dressed in 'mannish attire', never married and instead embarked upon intensely emotional relationships with women such as the poet Mary Robinson has been interpreted by critics as a sign of a lesbian sexual orientation on Lee's part (Colby, 52). Martha Vicinus, for example, has cited both Lee's insistence in her 1884 novel *Miss Brown* on the socially productive lives that women who consciously refused (heterosexual) marriage could live and extant letters between Lee and firstly, Mary Robinson and later, her successor in Lee's affections, Kit Anstruther-Thomson, as evidence of Lee's lesbianism.[2] And here, it is also worth noting that Lee's fellow cultural historian John Addington Symonds suggested Lee and Robinson's relationship to the sexologist Havelock Ellis as a case study for the section on lesbianism they were writing for their co-authored study about homosexuality *Sexual Inversion* (1897).[3] Conversely, Christa Zorn has found the application of a single lesbian identity to Lee to be reductive and suggests that 'Any critical accounts of Vernon Lee's lesbian orientation call for cautious attention' and that 'we need to see her lesbianism ... as one of the many contingencies that shape her "difference" as a writer and critic' (Zorn, 23). And, in their introduction to a recent collection of essays on Lee's work, Catherine Maxwell and Patricia Pulham have shown how in her fiction 'Lee represents sexual desire as complex, violent, contradictory, and perverse, cryptically expressed through personae who dramatize but are often themselves unable to

2

apprehend their own erotic drives and impulses'. 'Same-sex desire in particular,' they continue, 'is often represented obliquely, fractured, split or shifting between ostensibly hetero-sexual characters, caught in ambiguous triangular relation-ships'.[4]

According to Hilary Fraser, another formative contingency that shaped Lee's subject position was her complex national identity and the cosmopolitan sensibility that this produced. Fraser describes Lee as 'an Englishwoman born in France, who spent most of her life in Italy and wrote principally on Italian and British culture' and gauges the impact that this European identity had on her writing. For Fraser, both the postcolonial critic Homi Bhabha's theorization of 'borderline identities' and Stuart Hall's work on 'in-between' subjectivities have proved insightful in recuperating the creative influence that Lee's dislocated national identity exercised over her work. Fraser applies the terms of Stuart Hall's 1995 essay 'New Cultures for Old' to show how Lee's interstitial national identity allowed her to 'unsettl[e] the assumptions of one culture from the perspective of another' and contemporaneously made her 'both the *same as* and at the same time *different from*' the culture in which she lived.[5]

As we see throughout this study, a simultaneous sense of intimacy and alienation informs Lee's response to both British and European culture. Lee wrote of the benefit that her nomadic upbringing in France, Switzerland and Germany and her education at the hands of various European governesses had had in bringing her into intimate contact with various countries.[6] Her travel-writing is often wistful and impressionis-tic, sometimes dwelling on fond childhood memories of obscure places she had once visited. The intimate emotional connection that Lee forged with various European places and localities led her to style herself a 'sentimental traveller' (see Colby, 249). In her 1899 description of Augsburg, Germany, for example, Lee is careful to distinguish between modern militaristic Germany which, in her words, 'colonises ... or frightens the rest of the world in various ways' and the Germany that 'invented Christmas-trees, and Grimm's Fairy Tales, and Bach, and Mozart' (*GL*, 13). Yet as often as Lee presented herself in an emotional and affective communion with the spirit or 'genius loci' of places in Europe, equally she expressed anxiety that her expatriate identity kept her perpetually aloof and marginalized from the cultures she was writing about. Her ghost stories often centre on unnerving European encounters in which highly-strung and neurotic modern narrators are haunted by spectres from a country's past. And finally, the events of the First World War politicized Lee's cosmopolitan identity irrevocably. While in the newspaper articles and plays that she wrote against the war Lee argued that her special relationship to Europe had conferred upon her the ability to see the war from all angles, her opinions were widely viewed as unpatriotic by the majority of her British and European readers.

Lee's life in letters was also shaped by the often fractious friendships that she had with celebrated male writers of the day such as Walter Pater, J.A. Symonds, Oscar Wilde, Henry James, and H.G. Wells. Lee's most recent biographer Vineta Colby has described how her 'unchallenged authority as a writer on Italian culture' meant that from the 1880s onwards, she could leave her parental home in Italy to pay regular unchaperoned visits to friends such as Mary Robinson in London (Colby, 1). Although their mother's modest private income meant that neither Lee nor her brother ever depended upon their writing for money, nonetheless, Lee was eager to secure professional associations with London's literary *cognoscenti* on her annual visits to the city. Laurel Brake has written of how Lee 'strategically dedicated' her work to established writers such as Walter Pater and Henry James in order to 'anchor and authenticat[e] herself in English letters'.[7] In the first chapter, I explore the ramifications of such associations, particularly her dedication of her satirical novel, about high art in London, *Miss Brown*, to Henry James. Despite these strategic dedications, however, Maxwell and Pulham suggest that the manner in which Lee disseminated her writing, particularly her non-fiction work, was not to prove commercially successful. They argue that Lee's decision to place her essays in prestigious periodicals such as the *Cornhill* and the *Contemporary Review* rather than immediately present them in book form impacted negatively on sales (*HAOFT*, 'Introduction', 9–10). Furthermore, Lee's interest in writing works on psychology and music at the beginning of the twentieth century and her outspoken pacifism also reduced her readership further. Yet, as we shall see, throughout her career Lee managed to respond productively to her lack of an audience and the study concludes with a discussion of *The Handling of Words* (1924), her collected lectures on the art of good writing, in which she sought to tutor modern audiences in the best reading practices and, by extension, improve the state of literature in the post-war period.

Another formative influence that impacted upon Lee's life and work was her life-long struggle to achieve both physical health for herself and to promote artistic 'health' more generally amongst her contemporaries. In 1873, Eugene succumbed to what appears to have been a psychosomatic illness that was to leave him paralysed for twenty years and she and her mother were in constant attendance. Lee, herself, suffered from sustained bouts of neuralgia and nervous depression after the collapse of her relationship with Mary Robinson in 1888. In a letter written in 1894, Lee seemed to intimate that it was her mother's influence and the pressure of the intellectual ambitions that she had nursed for her from an early age that had led to the uneven psychological tenor of her adult life. Lee wrote to her friend the Italian writer Carlo Placci:

> I recognise that my family is, on one side, acutely neuropathic and hysterical; and that my earlier years were admirably calculated, by an alternation of indiscipline and terrorism, by excessive overwork and absolute solitude, to develop these characteristics. Had I known this at 22 or 23, instead of learning nearer forty, I should now be a good deal sounder and happier'. (quoted in Colby, 2)

That many of Lee's critical works assert the importance of cultivating a state of mental and physical serenity in order to achieve individual well-being, reveal the extent to which her personal experience of her own and other's ill-health directly impacted upon her writing. For example, in an early essay on the work of the critic John Ruskin, Lee argued that what she perceived as Ruskin's asceticism had had the negative effect of 'warp[ing]' his simple appreciation of beauty (*B*, 201).[8] As we shall see in the first chapter, Lee would spend the tumultuous decade of the 1890s publicly counselling the avant-garde school of the Aesthetic Movement that art should not be the instrument of 'intellectual rebellion and lawlessness', but rather that it was the duty of artists to produce healthy and morally educative art, in order to actively allay the fears of cultural and social decline promulgated by contemporary conservative commentators such as the German philosopher Max Nordau in his (in)famous book *Degeneration* (1893) (*GA*, 14). Between 1888 and 1912, Lee also experimented with the notion that classical art could literally induce good health in her research into the 'scientific' field of 'psychological aesthetics'. And, the final chapter of this study explores how in this somewhat eccentric project Lee and her collaborator Kit Anstruther–Thomson sought to prove that mimicking the poses of classical Greek statues would heighten the viewer's muscular strength, improve his or her posture and ultimately harmonize the body into a state of well-being.

Vernon Lee lived through a time of immense change. As she astutely recognized in her second pacifist play *Satan the Waster* (1920), European nations had had the potential at the turn of the twentieth century to develop a new global and truly universal consciousness but, according to her, had ultimately misused their contact with foreign peoples and cultures for the purposes of exploitation and imperial expansion. She also lamented the fact that first-world imperialism had been accompanied by the rise of narrow, violent and irrational nationalist movements in Europe, and that modern technological innovation had not brought nations into a more sympathetic relationship with each other but had seemingly only made mass slaughter more efficient (*SW*, xxxvi–xxxvii, 77–8; *GA*, 85). Where she had once believed that modern man was 'better' than his predecessors because the people of the past 'had, apparently no imagination for other folks' anguish', the events of the First World War and the incipient destruction of her beloved Europe made her question just how empathetic twentieth-century man actually was (*GL*, 43–4).

This introductory study attempts to relay something of Vernon Lee's expansive and scholarly interests in subjects such as art, European cultural history and the social and economic position of women and examines how she conveyed these ideas in the inventive and impassioned fiction and drama that she wrote. The study is broadly chronological and opens by positioning Lee's fiction of the 1880s and 1890s in relation to the high art movements of the day. Chapter 1 examines how artistic personalities such as Dante Gabriel Rossetti and Oscar

Wilde and the 'progressive' principles that they propounded informed Lee's ethical, sexual and aesthetic politics. In the second chapter, Lee's use of the short story form is examined and I consider how her cosmopolitan outlook was to inspire some of her most experimental writing in this genre. Finally, in chapter 3 some of the more controversial and groundbreaking works that Lee produced after the *fin de siècle* are explored. As the critical resurrection of this cosmopolitan intellectual and independent woman writer continues to gather pace, it seems that Vernon Lee still has much to say to twenty-first century readers on topics such as art's role in fostering the ethical and political evolution of society, gender inequality, globalization and war. And, it is my hope that the reader will give this pioneering and courageous writer the sympathetic and responsive hearing that she continually pursued throughout her career and most certainly deserved.

1

Vernon Lee and 'High Art'

Vernon Lee made her entrance into English letters at a time when radical artists in Britain were challenging what they considered to be the moral orthodoxy, numbing materialism and conservative artistic tastes of Victorian society. From the so-called 'Fleshly Controversy' of 1871 to the violent public backlash against British Decadent art and artists that accompanied the prosecution of Oscar Wilde for gross indecency in 1895, the final decades of the nineteenth century witnessed heated debates: in the press, in literature and, on a few memorable occasions, in court between proponents of high art like the Pre-Raphaelite Brotherhood (PRB), writers and critics such as John Ruskin who *conversely* maintained that beauty had a moral and spiritual imperative to fulfil *and* an avowedly philistine and increasingly hostile public.[1]

Accordingly, much of the fiction that Lee wrote in the 1880s and 1890s was formed by, and responded to, prevalent cultural debates about the morality and permissiveness of high art. Works such as Lee's first novel *Miss Brown* (1884), the novella *A Phantom Lover* (1886; reprinted as 'Oke of Okehurst; Or, The Phantom Lover' in 1890) and her Decadent fairytale 'Prince Alberic and the Snake Lady' (1896) relayed her unique vision of the ethical and moral problems posed both by the literary avant-garde *and* the public reaction to it. In her fiction and her essays of this period, not only did Lee ask challenging questions about the artist's responsibility to his audience in terms of both the content and moral meaning of his work but more bravely she also asked the late-Victorian public to look beyond its ingrained prejudices and see whether anything that might benefit or improve society could be learned from the revolutionary ideas propounded by this so-called 'new school' of artists (GA, 74).

Since the inception of the PRB in 1848 and despite the speedy dissolution of the group, both the work and unconventional personal lives of its founding members (William Morris, William Holman Hunt, John Everett Millais, Edward Burne Jones and Dante Gabriel Rossetti) continued to scandalize society for many years.[2] In 1871, poems by Rossetti appeared for the first time in one volume and occasioned a powerful public attack from the poet and critic Robert Buchanan in his infamous review article 'The Fleshly School of Poetry: Poems by D. G. Rossetti' for the *Contemporary Review*. In it, Buchanan castigated the poets Rossetti and Charles Algernon Swinburne for consciously abandoning themselves to sensuality in their work (thus, earning themselves the 'fleshly' moniker) and writing poems that he found to be 'affected', 'outrageous' and 'blasphemous'. Even more troubling for public morals, Buchanan argued, was the fact that such poetry was not the mere outpourings of a youthful imagination but was intentionally the work of mature poets.[3]

In many ways, Buchanan's accusations against the 'Fleshly School' of unbridled sexual indulgence and irreligious tendencies laid the ground for later charges of hedonism and paganism which would be levelled at Britain's next generation of radical artists, the Aesthetic Movement. Self-styled aesthetes (most notably Oscar Wilde) took their inspiration from the essays on the art of the Renaissance, *The Renaissance: Studies in Art and Poetry* (1873), written by the Oxford scholar and cultural historian, Walter Pater. Provocatively, in this collection of essays on the Renaissance artists, Joachim du Bellay, Luca della Robbia, Leonardo da Vinci, Michaelangelo, Botticelli and Pico Della Mirandola, Pater appeared to reject any sense that art should be a vehicle for moral teaching and clearly signalled that pleasure should be the final measure of all experience. Even more disquieting for Victorian readers was an essay on the eighteenth-century antiquarian Johann Joachim Winckelmann that Pater included in *The Renaissance*, in which he praised Winckelmann's appreciation for the beautiful representations of the male form in classical Greek sculpture. Worryingly, this essay seemed not only to align itself to a pagan and amoral system of ethics but even more controversially appeared homoerotic in outlook. Pater's reputation at Oxford was damaged both by the reception of the book and the discovery of compromising letters he had written to a male student and yet, when compared with the febrile atmosphere of the 1890s, the *public* critiques of the Aesthetic Movement in its early days were relatively mild. Pater was lampooned as the effete 'Mr Rose' by his former student W.H. Mallock in his popular novel *The New Republic* (1877), Wilde was regularly caricatured by George Du Maurier in the satirical periodical *Punch* as the poets 'Jellaby Posthlethwaite', 'Oscurio Wildegoose' and 'Drawit Milde' and, in Gilbert and Sullivan's highly successful comic opera *Patience* (1881), Aesthetes were satirized for their excessive devotion to beauty and laughable attempts to overhaul conventional morality. On a decidedly more serious and darker note, in his critically acclaimed novel *The Portrait of a Lady* (1880, 1881) the expatriate American novelist Henry James criticized aestheticism for encouraging attitudes of social detachment and a sterile connoisseurship in its adherents. And in the 1890s, the Aesthetic Movement went on to acquire a new and more disturbing demeanour in the influence that French Decadent writing was beginning to exercise over British artists such as George Moore, Oscar Wilde and Lionel Johnson (to name but a few) who, as exemplified by Wilde's novel *The Picture of Dorian Gray* (1890; 1891), began to import the variously mystical, ornate and sordid aspects of this literature into their own.

Initially, as we can see in her 1881 essay on Ruskin's criticism ('Ruskinism') Lee, rejected the critic's influential pronouncements on the moral and religious function of beauty, and thereby aligned herself with the controversial principles of the so-called 'art for art's sake' movements. In it, she writes:

> Beauty, in itself, is neither morally good nor morally bad: it is aesthetically good, even as virtue is neither aesthetically good nor aesthetically bad, but morally good. Beauty is pure, complete, egotistic: it has no other value than its being beautiful. (*B*, 210)

However, Lee began to reconsider this early commitment to 'aesthetic' principles when she visited London for the first time in the summer of 1881 at the invitation of Mary Robinson and was introduced to the actual proponents and supporters of high art. Her letters home to her mother veer between lively vignettes of the literary lions of London she met, including Robert Browning, Walter Pater, Oscar Wilde and William Morris, and her increasing frustration and exasperation at the posturing of Pre-Raphaelite and aesthetic artists and their followers. On visiting an exhibition of new works at the Royal Academy in 1881 she described the fashionable artistic-set who were gathered there to her mother:

> All the exhibition rooms were thrown open & crammed with people more or less artistic fashionable. I never saw so many shabby or insane dresses & so few pretty women in my life. I was quite astounded coming out, to see so many grand carriages. The dresses didn't look at all on a par with them. There were some crazy looking creatures: one with crinkled gauze all tied close about her & visibly no underclothes (& gold laurel wreath)...another with trimming and necklace of marigolds & parsley fern on thread, a lot of insane slashing & stomachings.[4]

Lee reserved her particular criticism for Pre-Raphaelite art and artists. She unkindly portrayed the painter and poet William Morris as a 'thickset shockhaired, bearded man, powerful, common, rather like a railway porter or bargee' and described Rossetti's paintings as not 'merely ill painted and worse modelled, but coarse and repulsive' (VLL, 70). However, her response to Pater and Wilde was decidedly more sympathetic. While at first, she thought Pater 'dull' and 'lymphatic' she was pleased by the attention that his sisters had shown her on her visit (VLL, 78–9). This first meeting led to a lasting friendship in which, between the years 1881 and 1884, she and Pater corresponded regularly about their work and Lee continued to visit the Pater family until 1891.

Lee also felt a particular, if unspoken affinity, with Oscar Wilde; after meeting him she wrote to her mother:

> The wonderful Oscar Wilde was brought up – the Postlethwaite of Punch. I must send you a caricature of him. He talked a sort of lyrico-sarcastic maudlin cultschah [sic] for half an hour. But I think the creature is clever, & that a good half of his absurdities are mere laughing at people. The English don't see that. (VLL, 65)

Vineta Colby speculates that Lee's sense of a special understanding of Wilde lay in her 'quickly detect[ing] the satire [Wilde]...was directing at the humorless aesthetes of Pre-Raphaelitism' (Colby, 80). Lee was also amused by Gilbert and Sullivan's comic opera Patience but its very success seemed to her to show that by 1881 'art for art's sake' was already passé. Lee

11

saw the opera in Oxford that summer and again wrote to her mother that the piece 'takes off aesthetic, high art people, but aestheticism it seems, except at Mr Gosse's (who receives his guests in ginger velveteen & red slippers) has wellnigh died out in London' (*VLL*, 77). This sense of the demise of the movement was to prove premature and, at any rate, did not prevent her from writing her own satirical novel, *Miss Brown*, about it three years later.

FLESHLY MATTERS: *MISS BROWN*

While, as seen above, exposing the peccadilloes of high art circles was certainly not uncommon, what marks *Miss Brown* out from other critiques of a similar ilk is that the novel offers a candid exploration of issues that touched Lee deeply in both the areas of her professional and personal life. Thus the novel explores the anomalies marking the sexual politics of radical artistic circles, the limited educational and vocational opportunities which faced all women, regardless of their class, and her passionate belief in the new and positive role that women who, like herself, rejected marriage and motherhood could play in improving society. Although, at points, the novel might discomfort the modern reader with injunctions against radical art that echo Buchanan's hostile position in the decade-old 'Fleshly Controversy', perhaps more surprising to the modern mind is the way that contemporary reviewers accused Lee of 'fleshliness' herself. One unsigned reviewer for the *Spectator* wrote that 'We cannot review this book at the length its powers would justify, the subject being too repulsive' and continued damningly that the novel 'exaggerates the area of the sexual question in life'. The numerous accusations of prurience that Lee faced from her reviewers induced a severe crisis in confidence in herself and her writing. 'Here I am accused of having, in simplicity of heart, written, with a view to moralise the world, an immoral book', she reflected that winter, 'accused of having done more mischief by setting my readers' imagination hunting up evil, than I possibly could do good by calling on their sympathies to hate that mischief' (quoted in Colby, 109–10).

Lee's fictional tale of how a young maidservant, the exotic half-Italian half-Scottish beauty Anne Brown, is discovered in

Italy by a famous Pre-Raphaelite artist, the 'handsome, effeminate, æsthetic aristocrat' painter Walter Hamlin, and is educated and introduced to London's fashionable high-art society by him seems (and certainly was taken to be) closely modelled on real-life events and personalities (*MB*, 1: 176). As with satires such as *Patience* and Du Maurier's satirical sketches in *Punch*, Lee's novel takes a broad swipe at high art. By heading up a band of Aesthetes, writing a sonnet sequence dedicated to 'desire' and painting pictures with 'gemlike harmonies of colour', Lee's fictional Walter Hamlin is clearly intended to recall Dante Gabriel Rossetti who had died two years previously (*MB*, 1:5). Miss Brown appears to be a composite character based on two real-life Pre-Raphaelite models: Elizabeth Siddal, Rossetti's wife and a painter in her own right, and Jane Morris, the wife of William Morris. Like these two women, Miss Brown comes from a working-class background, is introduced to society by her artist lover and ascends to the status of Pre-Raphaelite icon; moreover her monumental and statuesque beauty physically recalls that of Jane Morris. Amongst other aesthetic personalities, the novel also offers a thinly disguised caricature of Oscar Wilde in the figure of the 'elephantine' poet Posthlethwaite, a name which refers to Du Maurier's well-known sketches of Wilde in *Punch* (*MB*, 2:8).

While Lee had been shocked at the accusations of prurience levelled at her, she also appears to have misjudged how offensive her caricatures of London's high art personalities would prove, as the novel so upset Wilde, the Morrises and others that they avoided any social contact with her for many years. In light of the prestige that she had enjoyed as a highbrow writer following the publication of *Studies of the Eighteenth Century in Italy* which initially made Lee recoil from the idea of writing a novel, her eventual decision to do so (and a popular, satirical one at that) was also judged a mistake.[5] For example, Henry James, whom she had consulted in the novel's planning stages and to whom, much to his embarrassment, she dedicated *Miss Brown* was under the impression that Lee intended to write 'a very radical and aesthetic' novel (quoted in Gunn, 103). After a five-month silence, he eventually wrote to Lee with his opinion of the book and, like other reviewers, revealed his discomfort at what he perceived to be the novel's fleshliness and prurience. James gently admonished Lee by telling her that she had been 'too savage' in her depiction of London's aesthetic 'painters... poets, and dilettanti' because, according to him, real life was 'less obnoxious, less objectionable, [and] less crude' than she had depicted it to be in the novel. He also felt that the novel's impassioned style showed that Lee had not achieved a proper sense of objective distance from her subject and, in order to write a better novel next time, he advised her to 'Cool first – write afterwards' because, according to him, 'Morality is hot – but art is icy'. Privately, his thoughts about Lee's skills as a novelist were decidedly less charitable as he described the novel to his correspondent T. S. Perry as 'very bad' and 'inferior' to Lee's other writing (quoted in Colby, 107–8).

In *Miss Brown,* Lee articulated her passionate antipathy to what she considered to be the pretentiousness, sexual hypocrisy and moral dissipation of the proponents and practitioners of high art in London. More pressingly, the novel exposes what Lee perceived to be the gender inequality at the heart of the Pre-Raphaelite movement by highlighting the disparity between the iconic status that the group accorded to female models such as Siddal and Jane Morris in paintings like Millais' *Ophelia* (1852) and Rossetti's *Beata Beatrix* (1863) *and* the lack of critical and creative autonomy actually allowed to them. (This point is reinforced by Gail Marshall's recent observation that even when Siddal exercised her artistic autonomy by producing her own work, her paintings were treated like a lesser version of Rossetti's.)[6] From the outset, Hamlin reads Anne as an exotically pagan but lifeless aesthetic object. To him, she appears to be 'no living creature, but some sort of strange statue... a beautiful and sombre idol of the heathen' (*MB,* 1:24). Hamlin again later uses the sculptural metaphor to invoke the mythic trope of 'Pygmalion and Galatea' which Lee deploys to underscore the essential chauvinism with which male Pre-Raphaelite artists treated their female muses.[7] Hamlin considers how:

> instead of [his life]...being a mere possible, but by no means probable, instrument of a change in her [Anne's] life, she was the predestined instrument for the consummation of his life. Anne Brown should live for the world and for fame; and Walter Hamlin's life should be crowned by gradually endowing with vitality, and then wooing, awakening the love of this beautiful Galatea whose

soul he had moulded, even as Pygmalion had moulded the limbs of the image which he had made to live and to love. (*MB*, 1:121–2)

Marshall has shown the special currency that the Pygmalion and Galatea myth had for Victorian male artists because of the way in which it offered a mythic paradigm for the artist's mastery of his female subject.[8] She suggests that for Victorian Pygmalions the living statue 'remains only and always the image of Pygmalion's desire. Galatea literally bodies forth that desire, and the ultimate derivation of her being Venus restricts her to a range of purely physical representations' (Marshall, 18). Lee's Pygmalion (Hamlin) believes that Anne has no subjectivity until he grants her one and, as we see in the passage above, it is one that promises to do no more than narcissistically 'body forth' (to use Marshall's evocative phrase) his own desire. Hamlin believes that by paying for, and directing, Anne's education he will have accorded her a mind where he casually assumes that she previously did not have one. His plan to bring her to appreciate his work is one that rebounds spectacularly upon him.

At school, Anne reads letters from Hamlin in which, as her mentor, he recommends works of 'Greek lyrism, Oriental mysticism, French æstheticism, but above all, things medieval and pseudo-medieval' while, as a suitor, he writes of 'mysterious temptations of unspeakable things, beckoning his nobler nature into the mud, which he never at all specified'. Anne's initial innocence means that in the poetry that Hamlin writes and sends to her she finds that she 'did not always understand exactly the things to which he alluded, seeing only the beauty, the vague passionate wistfulness, the delicate sadness of what he wrote' (*MB*, 1: 226, 1: 224). She is quickly disabused of her naïvety when she comes into social contact with Hamlin's followers in London. Ironically, it is through the very education and experience that Hamlin allows her that Anne comes to gain a full understanding of his mind, as he had hoped she would. However, instead of passively mirroring his desire back to him like her mythical counterpart, Anne is so pained by the 'improper' and 'impure' works produced by him and his circle that she seeks to reform them (*MB*, 1: 295 and 2: 87).

Through her depiction of Anne Brown's growing independence, Lee challenges the conventions of male mastery and female passivity incarnated in the most powerful trope to govern

15

relations between male artists and the female muse across the nineteenth century. In Lee's recasting of the myth, Galatea speaks and seeks to mould her Pygmalion. Under the new moral influence that Anne exerts over him, Hamlin is persuaded to try and write a different kind of poetry. Lee writes:

> It was beginning to be obvious, to every one who was not an æsthete, that the reign of the mysterious evil passions...must be coming to a close; and that a return to nature must be preparing. Anne had felt it, and had vaguely determined that the man who was to revolutionise poetry was Hamlin. (*MB*, 2: 71–2)

Anne's hopes that Hamlin will abandon fleshly improprieties in order to 'revolutionise poetry' and regenerate art through a return to Nature as its subject-matter prove to be short-lived.

To Anne's relief, Hamlin uses a holiday in the country away from the salons of aesthetic London to write a long poem, 'The Ballad of the Fens'. The poem has a Wordsworthian pastoral setting and foregoes the usual dark passions with which his school is associated and, instead, celebrates sanguine domestic pleasures. While Miss Brown approves of this new poetic vision, Hamlin's set cannot accept that their leader has abandoned the old style. The ghost of the decade-old 'Fleshly Controversy' is reanimated when the judgements the group offer on the new ballad confirm the accusations of stylistic perversity, moral wrong-headedness and puerile naughtiness that Buchanan had made against the movement a decade earlier. The fictional Aesthetes' postures of immorality have so poisoned their view of the world that, perversely, they read scenes of domestic happiness as 'beastly'. Significantly, under pressure from the group's disgust over 'The Ballad of the Fens', Hamlin tears up the poem and abandons the new mode of poetic sincerity. The invidious influence of poets such as the 'rickety' Denistoun triumphs as Hamlin chooses to use Anne's real anxieties about the morally degraded condition to which poverty has reduced his tenants as poetic material and rewrites 'The Ballad of the Fens' as a dark naturalist poem about incest in the countryside (*MB*, 2:75).

Where Buchanan had warned that the Fleshly School had produced a number of imitators who were convinced that following their puerile formulas would make 'great poets' of them, in *Miss Brown*, Lee is equally concerned with the pressure that imitators exert on the master.[9] Significantly, at the decisive point of re-launching his career in a new direction and, by his example, saving the school from further ignominy, Hamlin is turned away from Anne's healthy influence by his followers. Moreover, Miss Brown also begins to consider the psychological damage that Hamlin and his circle's 'aesthetic selfishness' might have inflicted on her, since she feels that her proximity to the school has left her unable to trust her own judgement and she begins to wonder if 'all the impure poetry which she had lately been reading...might not be making her imagine things which were not meant' (*MB*, 2: 233, 2: 87). Equally disturbing to Miss Brown is that Hamlin's 'morbidly introspective and self-scrutinising, imaginative' poems are not expressions of real feelings he has experienced, as Buchanan had complained earlier of Rossetti and Swinburne, these are the carefully crafted and artificial works of a mature poetic mind specifically produced for public titillation (*MB*, 2: 89; Buchanan, 338–9). It is significant that Hamlin also defends the offending 'desire' sonnets by stating that 'Such things must be judged from a purely artistic standpoint' (*MB*, 2: 97). The belief of Hamlin's circle that art should not be beholden to conventional morality recalls both the aesthetic principles that Lee had recently abandoned and anticipates the public furore that would be caused by Oscar Wilde's Decadent novel about high art in London, *The Picture of Dorian Gray*, which, in its second edition, would also be prefaced by the provocative declaration that 'There is no such thing as a moral or immoral book'.[10]

Despite the 'fleshliness' and challenges to conventional sexual mores offered by Aesthetes and Pre-Raphaelites, the gender politics of these high art movements did not represent a serious intervention for Lee against the social and sexual inequalities marking relations between the sexes in the late-Victorian period. Lee shows that, as liberated and as permissive in attitude as these Aesthetes perceive themselves to be, in actuality their behaviour is hypocritical and beholden to the very values they rail against. This is seen where, in a fit of pique, Hamlin causes a temporary rift between Anne's friend Marjorie and her fiancé by intentionally and dishonestly accusing her of flirting with someone else.

Equally, *Miss Brown* also reveals Lee's pessimism with regards to the attitudes that political radicals adopted towards women. Through Anne's relationship with her cousin, the reform politician Richard Brown, we see how, in Lee's formulation, political radicals are as guilty as the Aesthetes of refusing women any autonomy and, more disappointingly, any vocation. Initially, Richard Brown appears to offer Anne refuge from the Aesthetes and their world as they discuss serious subjects together such as political economy and social reform. Anne begins to hope that she might leave the Aesthetes behind and share in Richard's projects, an idea that he encourages, but, much to her horror and disappointment, it turns out that his interest in her has been motivated by romantic feelings all along. Anne is disheartened to find that 'Richard Brown loved her, wanted her; it was the old nauseous story over again; the sympathy, the comradeship, the quiet brotherly and sisterly affection had all been a sham, a sham for her and for himself' (*MB*, 3: 75–6). (Here, Christa Zorn crisply observes that '[w]hen …[Lee] stages an encounter between aesthetic and socialist movements, neither comes out a winner, mainly because of the limited roles they offer women' (Zorn, xxx)). Through Anne's realization that Richard's interest in her is rooted in his sexual desire, Lee points out that in contemporary society, wherever a woman's vocational ambitions and aspirations might lie, her role is governed first and foremost by a reductive biological and sexual imperative. Significantly, this was precisely the reason that Lee would give in 1902 for never having written on the so-called 'Woman Question'. According to Lee this was because women were 'over-sexed'. She explains that:

> *Over-sexed* does not mean over-much addicted to sexual indulgence; very far from it, for that is the case not with women, but with men, of whom we do not say that they are *over-sexed*. What we mean by *over-sexed* is that, while men are a great many things besides being males – soldiers and sailors, tinkers and tailors, and all the rest of the nursery rhymes - women are, first and foremost *females*, and then – still more females. (*GA*, 281; emphases in original)

In her recognition of the failure of both radical (socialist) and high art circles to accommodate a woman's right to self-determination, Lee's sexual politics, as expressed in this novel, anticipate the kinds of critiques and tensions that various 'New

Women' writers would identify in both the attitudes of contemporary society and radical artists towards the 'Woman Question' over the next decade.[11]

Notwithstanding Lee's critique of the hypocrisy and affectation of the high art schools, the enshrining of unconventional figures of female beauty in Pre-Raphaelite art seems to have suggested to her that potentially high art carried within its artistic rubric the possibility of emancipating women from the conventional gender stereotypes that society forced upon them. To Hamlin, Anne is exceptional for the masculine bent of her beauty and his first vision of her offers a complex encoding of both aesthetic tropes and something curiously he has never seen before:

> The forehead was high and narrow, the nose massive, heavy, with a slight droop that reminded Hamlin of the head of Antinous;...He wondered as he looked at her; and wondered whether this strange type, neither Latin nor Greek, but with something of Jewish and something of Ethiopian subdued into a statuesque but most un-Hellenic beauty, had met him before. ...and as he looked at the girl, it seemed, despite its strangeness, as if, at some dim distant time, he had seen and known it well before. (*MB*, 1:25)

Hamlin reads Anne as a 'monumental' and universal figure who, significantly, is both sexually and racially 'other'. Strikingly, for him, she recalls statues of Antinous, the famed boy lover of the Roman Emperor Hadrian, and this comparison of Anne's beauty to that of a timeless homosexual boy icon opens up a number of possible interpretations of Anne's sexual identity. Significantly, Martha Vicinus, in her reading of two later stories by Lee, 'Prince Alberic and the Snake Lady' and 'A Wedding Chest', has argued for the special meaning of the figure of the boy in both male homosexual and lesbian literature. According to Vicinus, 'middle-class homosexual writers of both sexes shifted the focus to an idealized adolescent boy', and she continues that 'Even though many male homosexuals were not pederast and most lesbians did not look like boys, the boy was the defining free agent who best expressed who they were'.[12] In the context of *Miss Brown*, Lee's use of the Antinous metaphor is not clear, since it could equally encode a reference either to a latent homoeroticism on Hamlin's part or, if not a lesbian identity for Anne, then certainly a non-normative (heterosexual) one. What

19

is certain, however, is that from the outset Hamlin recognizes that even his sexually permissive aestheticism cannot encompass Anne's 'difference'. Indeed, her boyish beauty (her sexual difference) does not remain fixed but is quickly subsumed ('subdued') into figures of racial difference as Hamlin muses on Anne's 'Jewish', 'Ethopian', and 'un-Hellenic' beauty. Anne's beauty even appears to contest historical periodization as Hamlin both sees in it a new female archetype and yet also finds it to be timelessly iconic.

Hamlin's vision of Anne's unique beauty lays the ground for a momentous direct address on Lee's part to the reader where she propagandizes for an even more radical mode of femininity than that propounded by aesthetes. In an extended passage in volume 2 of the novel (307–9), Lee allows herself to speculate on what Anne could achieve in society if she realizes that being true to her essential nature makes it necessary for her to reject marriage and motherhood. Here, Lee places Anne in a sorority of 'women without woman's instincts and wants, sexless – women made not for man but for humankind' and envisages this non-normative female identity as potentially the site of dynamic social change. In this powerfully suggestive passage, Lee conceives of a new paradigm of female identity which prioritizes both what society refuses to give to women, a vocation, and resists what it enforces upon them, marriage and motherhood. To Lee, Anne's potential acceptance of her sexual difference is ennobling and the 'Joan[ ] of Arc' identity that she accords her heroine carries within it special powers to regenerate mankind (*MB*, 2: 308–9). We see Lee annexe the conventional gender stereotypes that emphasized woman's innate moral superiority over men, ideas which were propounded both by Victorian feminists and their critics, in order to articulate an unconventional gender identity for her exceptional heroine. Moreover, Lee is careful to stress that the refusal of maternity and marriage cannot masculinize a woman such as Anne because she believes that women are essentially (sexually) purer than men.[13] In this respect, Martha Vicinus's recent suggestion that Lee constructs an alternative gender identity for Anne as a *superior* third sex' proves particularly apposite (Vicinus, 156; emphasis in original). This appears to be a defining moment in the text because the urgency and impassioned manner in which Lee addresses the reader seems to relay an epiphany that she, herself, had had about the future. It would seem that for Lee, exceptional women whose moral purity and refusal to tie themselves to the binds of marriage would induce spectacular social change in this world of 'injustice...callousness, and evil' (*MB*, 2: 308). And, equally, one cannot help but feel that Lee was also undertaking some special pleading for her own decision to reject the over-determined roles that society accorded women.

REVENANT AESTHETICS: *A PHANTOM LOVER*

Both Vineta Colby and Kirsten MacLeod have argued that Lee's *volte-face* in deciding to write the popular novel *Miss Brown* was motivated by her desire to bring her anxieties about high art before a larger audience (Colby, 96; MacLeod 60, 64). In the reading of Lee's novella *A Phantom Lover* that follows, we will explore how she continued to develop her use of popular fiction as a medium for critiquing the ethics and aesthetics of the New Schools. First issued in 1886, the novella appeared in the comparatively cheap but historically sensationalist format of the 'shilling dreadful' and, was received by one Victorian reviewer as a successful attempt to capitalize on the public appetite for fictionalized 'eeri[e]' and 'morbid' (medical) case-histories that had been started a few months earlier with the publication of Robert Louis Stevenson's 'shilling shocker' *The Strange Case of Dr Jekyll and Mr Hyde*.[14] And yet perhaps even more arresting than Lee's apparent venture into the popular Gothic *per se*, is the way that *A Phantom Lover* links the unsettling vision of psychiatric hysteria and mania that it depicts to the art-philosophy of her friend and erstwhile mentor, Walter Pater, as it appeared (and Pater protested was misunderstood) in *The Renaissance, Studies in Art and Poetry*. Certainly, this aspect of the tale did not seem to have passed unnoticed in the Pater household because when Lee read the proofs to Pater and his sisters, she tellingly observed to her mother that 'they liked it, or pretended to do so'.[15]

Before exploring the tale in some detail, it is worth examining both the main ideas articulated in *The Renaissance*, and its reception by contemporary readers, in order to recoup the seminal influence it exercised over Lee and others in the final quarter of the nineteenth century. Recently, critics such as Laurel Brake, Vineta Colby, Stefano Evangelista, and Christa Zorn, have all explored the formative influence that Pater's work exercised over Lee. Zorn and Colby, in particular, have identified Lee's implicit reservations about the general moral tenor of Pater's work and her uneasiness about his gender politics.[16] In *The Renaissance*, Pater framed his essays on the lives of influential Renaissance artists with an introduction and conclusion that offered the reader a manifesto for a new model of art criticism. He asked his reader to think of himself as an 'aesthetic critic' who did not evaluate art with judgements based on received convention but as someone who would learn to 'know [his] ... own impression as it really is, to discriminate it, to realise it distinctly'. Nor did Pater confine this impressionist method to questions of art appreciation alone as he encouraged 'the aesthetic critic ... [to] regard[ ] all objects with which he has to do, all works of art, and the fairer forms of nature and human life, as powers or forces producing *pleasurable sensations*'. Even more controversially, Pater seemed to absolve the reader from any moral or ethical responsibility to his wider community since, according to him, 'The theory or idea or system which requires of us the sacrifice of any part of this experience, in consideration of some interest into which we cannot enter, or some abstract theory we have not identified with ourselves, or of what is only conventional, has no real claim upon us'. For many commentators, Pater's final pronouncement of *The Renaissance* that 'art comes to you proposing frankly to give *nothing* but the highest quality to your moments as they pass, and simply for those moments' sake' confirmed that he dangerously rejected any sense that art should be a vehicle for moral teaching.[17]

In the influential essay on the artist Leonardo Da Vinci that appeared in *The Renaissance*, Pater imparted his thoughts on the meaning of Da Vinci's portrait *The Mona Lisa* (1503–06). Strikingly, he read *La Gioconda* as a disquieting figure whose beauty he found to be of an entirely different type from the classical beauties of Greek sculpture which were favoured in the Renaissance period. To Pater, hers was a beauty 'wrought ... of strange thoughts and fantastic reveries and exquisite passion' that was 'expressive of what in the ways of a thousand years men had come to desire'. He envisioned *The Mona Lisa* as a timeless and unsettling figure in whose image he could trace the imprint of successive epochs of immorality in Western culture and the portrait appeared to him to be an inscrutable Gothic enigma who 'like the vampire ... has been dead many times, and learned the secrets of the grave'. But to Pater she was more than a dangerous *femme fatale* because for him the 'Lady Lisa' embodied a particular philosophical meaning in which she incarnated both the ancient Greek philosopher Heraclitus's 'fancy of a perpetual life, sweeping together ten thousand experiences' and also 'modern philosophy['s]' conception of 'the idea of humanity as wrought upon by, and summing up in itself, all modes of thought and life' To Pater, the portrait seemed to tell of how each individual life was the sum of all lives preceding it and whose destiny was shaped by this collective experience (Pater, 79–80).

One critic hostile to Pater's work was George Eliot who found the book 'quite poisonous in its false principles of criticism and false conception of life.' This would be seconded by a former student and now colleague of Pater's at Oxford University, John Wordsworth, who wrote to him aghast at his philosophy (to quote Wordsworth), 'that no fixed principles of religion or morality can be regarded as certain [and] that the only thing worth living for is momentary enjoyment'. Wordsworth was particularly anxious about the effect that Pater's apparent call to an unorthodox life of sensual gratification would have on 'minds weaker than ... [his] own' (quoted in Colby, 60–1).

The Renaissance was to exercise a powerful hold on a generation of young writers such as Oscar Wilde, Arthur Symons, George Moore, Richard Le Gallienne and W. B. Yeats, who declared Pater their 'Master' and, in response to the principles articulated in his 'gospel of beauty and "ecstasy"', developed their own brand of high art as the Aesthetic Movement over the next two decades.[18] Pater's essay on Leonardo Da Vinci and his interpretation of the painting *The Mona Lisa* was to prove particularly inspirational to the movement (Wilde, 1126). Initially, Lee appeared to signal her affinity to Pater's art-philosophy by strategically dedicating her 1884 collection of essays on Renaissance culture, *Euphorion,* to him.

She highlighted her overt deployment of an impressionist method in it by characterizing her essays as 'mere impressions developed by means of study... currents of thought and feeling in myself, which have found and swept along with them certain items of Renaissance lore. For the Renaissance has been to me... not so much a series of studies as a series of impressions' (*E*, 1: 16). And yet, the intellectual kinship with Pater evinced here appears incongruous in light of the implicit moral criticism of impressionist historiography that Lee went on to offer in this study. Thus, Lee pointedly disapproved of the 'Dramatic emotion... [the] egotistic... [and] half-artistic pleasure' which was becoming the mainstay of 'history, and [which] the history especially of the Renaissance, has been made to pander but too much' (*E*, 1:12–13). And after Pater's death in 1894, Lee reviewed his legacy in the 'Valedictory' that she wrote to him in 1895. In it, she recalled the public reception of *The Renaissance* and how it had left in all 'sane persons' an impression of 'caducity and barrenness' and how its hedonistic principles 'must... result in a crumbling away of all such possible unity and efficiency of living', and yet equally she was also careful to emphasize how Pater's ensuing career saw him evolve from 'an aesthete and end[ ] as a moralist' (*RFS*, 255–7).

In *A Phantom Lover*, Lee conveys her ambivalent response to the art-philosophy that Pater propounded in *The Renaissance* in the form of an unconventional ghost story in which the reader is led to doubt seriously whether the protagonists have actually come into contact with the supernatural at all. Set in a beautiful Jacobean country house, the tale is narrated by a fashionable London portrait painter who recalls his disastrous encounter with an aristocratic couple who hire him one summer to paint them. On first meeting Mr Oke, the unnamed artist claims to have immediately recognized the physical marker of mental imbalance in his subject in the form of what a 'mad-doctor' friend of his calls a 'maniac-frown'. However, a more captivating and insidious form of 'psychological mania' presents itself to the painter in the behaviour of Oke's wife whose absolute identification with a seventeenth-century ancestress (another Alice Oke) confounds the painter. He also quickly realizes that Alice's obsession with the tragic love affair that took place between this ancestress and the Cavalier poet Lovelock, which ended in his murder, dangerously unnerves her husband. While the doctors have diagnosed Mrs Oke as suffering from a 'nervous constitution', the painter alternatively reads Alice Oke's behaviour as the caprice of a young woman who, it appears to him, has consciously fashioned herself in the 'aesthetic' mould (*HAOFT*, 108, 122, 110).

In her reading of the tale, Patricia Pulham briefly observes that Alice Oke's '"uncanny smile", her "exotic" elegance and "marvellous fantastic kind of grace" recall the figure of Pater's *La Gioconda*.[19] And yet, as argued below, this tale seems to offer more than a simple allusion to Pater's reading of *The Mona Lisa* but rather, as we shall see, expressly uses this figure (and aspects of *The Renaissance*, more generally) as a platform from which Lee launched a powerful critique of the sexual politics and ethics of the contemporary Aesthetic Movement. The painter, an 'aesthetic critic' *par excellence*, himself, uses an overtly Paterian vocabulary to describe Alice Oke. Like the enigmatic and impenetrable *Mona Lisa*, she is seen by the painter as 'the most marvellous creature' with 'a wonderful elegance, exotic, far-fetched, poignant'. And again, in line with Pater's reading of *La Gioconda*, the painter also accords Mrs Oke a timelessly iconic status. He muses that 'It is conceivable, is it not, that once in a thousand years there may arise a combination of lines, a system of movements, an outline, a gesture, which is new, unprecedented, and yet hits off exactly our desires for beauty and rareness'. Moreover, his confident announcement that 'I am very susceptible to such impressions...the sort of spasm of imaginative interest sometimes given to me by certain rare and eccentric personalities' appears to be a response to that privileging of subjective experience authorized by Pater's inspirational call to 'know one's own impression as it really is' (*HAOFT*, 106, 114, 112; Pater, xxix). The painter's absolute faith in his reading of Alice Oke makes him doubt 'whether anyone ever understood Alice Oke', the subject of his aesthetic vision, 'besides myself'.

Despite such confident pronouncements, Lee is careful to show how his perspective on events is entirely coloured by his total absorption in his self-appointed role as an 'aesthetic critic' of the Paterian school. She emphasizes how the painter is quickly overcome by the dream-like atmosphere of Okehurst

Manor and how he luxuriates in the 'special kind of voluptuous-ness, peculiar and complex and indescribable, like the half-drunkenness of opium or haschisch' that this 'palace of the Sleeping Beauty' induces. Inebriated with his own sensations, the painter pursues Alice Oke's 'physical image, her psychological explanation, with a kind of passion which filled [his]... days'. Yet his feelings soon turn to frustration when he realizes that this 'superior flirt' is absolutely indifferent to him. His realization that Mrs Oke barely registers his presence leads him to change his attitude towards her and he claims that he no longer trusts Mrs Oke and that 'That woman would slip through my fingers like a snake if I attempted to grasp her elusive character' (*HAOFT*, 107, 111–2, 117, 147). Here, the evocation of the snake simile places Mrs Oke in a genealogy of *femme fatales* associated with snake iconography: Eve, the Medusa, Cleopatra, and 'lamias'. (Sig-nificantly, in the 'Leonardo da Vinci' essay, Pater also described Da Vinci's *Medusa* as an 'interfusion of the extremes of beauty and terror' from whose head 'the delicate snakes seem [to be] literally strangling each other in terrified struggle to escape' (Pater, 67–8).) The artist's failure to master his modern *Mona Lisa* – symbolically, the portrait he is painting of Alice Oke remains unfinished and is a 'huge wreck' – generates a reaction on his part that implicitly figures her as an embodiment of an evil and destructive femininity (*HAOFT*, 106). In Lee's story, the painter's implicit positioning of Mrs Oke alongside Pater's vampiric 'Lady Lisa' is wholly represented as the construct of the frustrated male gaze. In Lee's depiction, the failure of a 'radical' masculine impressionism to incarcerate conclusively the female subject degenerates into anti-feminist diatribes.

In *Miss Brown*, Lee had questioned how successful the attempts of both Pre-Raphaelite artists and political reformers would be in reforming society as long as their sexual politics did not fully engage with the experiences of real women. Anne finds the aristocratic Hamlin and her reformer cousin Richard's attentions equally distasteful because whatever their political differences are, both men wish her to sacrifice her philanthropic vocation to their own sexual needs. Similarly in *A Phantom Lover*, Lee suggests that however radical high art circles perceive themselves to be in the dangerous and provocative images of women that they produce and promote, that essentially their gender politics are just as intractable and insensitive to women's needs as the values of the wider society which they seek to challenge. Indeed, when the painter realizes that he does not understand Alice as he thinks he does, his aesthetic fantasy begins to unravel and he falls back on, and even outdoes, the medical diagnoses that William Oke has been given by doctors to explain his wife's behaviour. To the painter, Alice's behaviour is no longer that of a Paterian temptress but is rather one of those 'extraordinary crazes of childless and idle women' (*HAOFT*, 122). Here, he espouses the conventional medical accounts of the kinds of mania and hysteria that the medical profession claimed resulted from a woman's failure to reproduce successfully. In *Passion and Pathology in Victorian Fiction*, Jane Wood notes how at the end of the Victorian period 'women were regularly being warned by socio-medical commentators in journals and periodicals that they were doubly disadvantaged since they courted nervous illness if they resisted their biological destiny of marriage and motherhood'.[20] It is ironic that when he cannot keep Alice Oke fixed in his reading of her not only does the painter judge her to be clinically insane but, like the contemporary medical profession, he reduces this woman to her reproductive function.

And yet as much as the husband and the artist attempt to fix the modern Alice Oke in contemporary categories of aberrant female behaviour (the hysteric, the flirt, the barren woman and the *femme fatale*), we see Alice Oke achieve temporary autonomy from both the clinical and aesthetic male gaze when she performs her version of Lovelock's murder by her ancestress. Here, rather than acquiescing to the painter's description of her, she is inspired to become a type of Paterian critic herself. At a family gathering, Alice Oke dresses as a groom, 'a boy, slight and tall' and offers her rendition in transvestite disguise of the infamous murder (*HAOFT*, 138). In this performance, we see her use this act of cross-dressing to both liberate herself from the passive *Mona Lisa* role she has been ascribed and assert her critical autonomy by appearing to respond to Pater's call for his reader to consider '[w]hat is this song or picture, this engaging personality presented in life or in a book, to *me*' (Pater, xxix). Here, it is significant, as she tells the painter, that her only proof that her ancestor committed Lovelock's murder rests in her belief that the story is true because she '*feels* it to be true' (*HAOFT*, 124; emphasis added).

Suggestively, the critic Richard Dellamora argued that, in his 'Winckelmann' essay, Pater envisioned the antiquarian as a type of *Mona Lisa* figure and that this transgender identification both 'impl[ies] the emancipation of women as well [as men]' and 'potentially... recognizes women's capacity both to *shape their own difference*, as well as for women to occupy the terrain of traditionally male gender roles'.[21] Thus through Alice Oke's narration of the murder in transvestite disguise it would seem that Lee responds to the inherent potential of Pater's work to articulate alternate sexual identities for women. Certainly, the critic Ruth Robbins asserts as much when she reads the 'diaphanous' figure of Mrs Oke as Lee's conscious exploitation of the gender indeterminacy of Pater's narrative figures to encode lesbian identity into the story (*HAOFT*, 123).[22] That the painter (the male Paterian) is deeply disconcerted by Alice Oke's cross-dressing and describes her performance as if he were in a 'madhouse' suggests that to him the only kinds of sexual dissidence and transgressive sexual identities that he finds acceptable are the ones that he subscribes to (*HAOFT*, 138). Ultimately, Lee's novella is pessimistic about how progressive Paterian principles are for women as Alice Oke's assertion of her personal autonomy through a liberating moment of transvestism only proves temporary. Despite the growing mania of her husband who, according to the painter, becomes 'perfectly unstrung, like a hysterical woman', Alice continues to insist upon the veracity of her impressions until Oke, convinced by her assertion that Lovelock haunts the house, accidentally kills her (*HAOFT*, 144). As with Anne Brown's self-sacrifice through her marriage to Hamlin which ultimately, Lee suggests, will fail to reform him, Alice Oke's untimely death again indicates that, for Lee, a woman's achievement of independence and articulacy within wider society was, under present conditions, only ever going to be temporary. We might also speculate that, through Alice Oke's transvestism, Lee was, in part, dramatizing the way in which she herself felt that she had to use a masculine pen-name as a professional cultural historian. Indeed, the way in which we see Alice Oke develop from a passive iconic figure constructed under the rubric of Pater's writing to an articulate woman who appropriates Paterian principles to assert (in Dellamora's terms) her *difference* for herself could, in part, also represent Lee's latent narration of her own progress from the role of Pater's erstwhile acolyte to a fully-fledged critic of his work.

Initially, by encouraging Mrs Oke in her 'harmless... eccentricity' and by failing to intervene in time to forestall her husband's growing mania, the painter's behaviour also indicates that, for Lee, the sense of social detachment that Pater had advocated in the 'Conclusion' to *The Renaissance* was dangerously irresponsible. Moreover, by using the name Oke (here, suggesting the English oak tree) and setting the novella in an English country house, Lee also intimates that aestheticism was anathema both to traditional English values and the national character. The painter patronizingly describes Oke as a 'type of the perfectly conscientious young Englishman... devout, pureminded, brave, incapable of any baseness, a little intellectually dense' and he tells of his frustration at the impossibility of getting 'this serious, conscientious, slow-brained representative of English simplicity and honesty and thoroughness to understand the mixture of self-engrossed vanity, of shallowness, of poetic vision, of love of morbid excitement, that walked this earth under the name of Alice Oke' (*HAOFT*, 122, 117, 140). Lee's prescience in staging a battle between aestheticism and traditional English values in this novella of 1886 is remarkable for anticipating the kind of violent distaste felt by the philistine public towards the Aesthetic Movement in the next decade. Indeed, to suggest, as Lee does in the novella, that the outcome of following aesthetic principles is madness and murder anticipates the pathologization of high art that would occur in the 1890s. In this decade, public hostility to the New Schools was fanned by the publication of another supernatural tale about aestheticism, Oscar Wilde's controversial novel *The Picture of Dorian Gray* in 1890 and, as we shall see below, the publication of the English translation of Max Nordau's pseudo-scientific work *Degeneration* in 1893 appeared to give scientific credence to such antipathy. With Wilde's prosecution in 1895, the public appeared to have final validation for its continued detestation of him and the artistic avant-garde. The final story examined in this chapter is Lee's fairytale 'Prince Alberic and the Snake

Lady' which was written in the direct aftermath of (in the words of one contemporary commentator) the 'orgy of Philstine rancour' that marked the Wilde trials.[23] In the reading that follows, we shall explore how this exotic fairytale attempts to persuade the public that after its initial ferment the Aesthetic Movement had matured and accrued strong ethical values. And yet, the deaths of both the fictional Prince and the Snake Lady ultimately suggest that for Lee the final triumph of philistine values in English culture could not be forestalled.

AN ETHICAL AESTHETICISM? 'PRINCE ALBERIC AND THE SNAKE LADY'

In 1893, in his immensely popular pseudo-scientific work *Degeneration*, the German philosopher Max Nordau portentously described the contemporary zeitgeist as a 'Dusk of the Nations' and warned against the disturbing spirit and corrupting influence which he believed a small minority of artistic and political radicals sought to exercise over wider society. For Nordau, the final decade of the nineteenth century had produced a generation of degenerates, hysterics and neurasthenics who lived, what he deemed to be, physically enervated and mentally aberrant existences under express direction from the social, political and literary 'fads' of the day. In his attack on contemporary avant-garde ideas, which ranged from the enlightened sexual politics of the Norwegian playwright Heinrik Ibsen to what he considered to be the provoking levity of the English aesthetes, Nordau systematically pathologized the radical theories of the so-called 'New Schools'. In this vein, he diagnosed the French poet Baudelaire's 'desperate cry towards the "new"' as 'the natural complaint of a brain which longs to feel the pleasure of action, and greedily craves a stimulation which his powerless sensory nerves cannot give him'. And while those 'degenerates' who considered themselves to be decidedly *fin de siècle* celebrated 'the richer vibrations of the refined nervous system of the present day' or laboured to give expression to 'the unknown sensations of an elect mind', Nordau declared his relief that, at least, 'The great majority of the middle and lower classes is not fin de siècle'.[24]

Two figures that came to particular prominence in the cultural landscape of the 1890s were the 'Decadent' and that late-Victorian feminist, the so-called 'New Woman'. Linda Dowling has shown how, although these two figures were diametrically opposed in their sexual politics and ethics, in the commitments to literary experimentation, and challenges to gender stereotypes and traditional institutions such as marriage and the family that the Decadent and the New Woman offered fixed them in the public mind (in Dowling's resonant phrase) as 'twin apostles of the social apocalypse'.[25] Conversely, for literary radicals the 'amazing decade' of the 1890s had a 'creative revolutionary energy' which brought writers such as W. B. Yeats, Arthur Symons, Ernest Dowson, Rudyard Kipling, H. G. Wells, and Robert Louis Stevenson to the fore (Le Gallienne, 78).

In his novel *The Picture of Dorian Gray* Wilde dramatized the slide of Pater's idealist aestheticism into what Kirsten MacLeod describes as 'the darker Aestheticism of Decadence' (MacLeod, 3). And as noted earlier, in the preface to his novel, Wilde offered the consciously provocative maxim that '[t]here is no such thing as a moral or an immoral book' and thereby suggested that art could only be judged from an artistic (rather than a moral) point of view. With its scenes of aristocratic criminality, drug-taking, extreme connoisseurship and (homo) sexual indiscretion, the novel pushed philistine hostility to high art schools to a new peak.[26] In 1895, the struggle between a philistine public and the literary avant-garde that had begun some twenty years earlier played out its tragic last act. That Wilde was prosecuted and subsequently imprisoned for acts of 'gross indecency' seemed to confirm public suspicions about the general 'immoral' tenor of the Aesthetic and Decadent movements. And yet, as becomes evident from newspaper reports and commentary of the trials it was not only Wilde's sexuality that was on trial but also the literary practices of the 'New Schools' now came under fire. John Stokes has noted how in the public mind Wilde had come to embody not only the total energies of the literary avant-garde (the so-called '"new school" in literature – the revolutionary and anarchist school') but even the sexual dissidence of the New Woman.[27] A mob rioted outside the offices of the publishers John Lane where the Decadent journal the *Yellow Book* (which was mistakenly associated in the public mind with Wilde) was published. Several newspaper editorials hoped that Wilde's downfall would forestall further artistic 'innovations' by radical artists and the *Daily Telegraph* expressed its hope that Wilde's 'removal will serve to clear the poisoned air, and make it cleaner for all healthy and unvitiated lungs.' In similar vein, an editorial in the *Evening News* addressed the young men who either associated with Wilde or appeared to model their behaviour on his with the hope that 'the conviction of Wilde for these abominable vices, which were the natural outcome of his diseased intellectual condition, will be a salutary warning to the unhealthy boys who posed as sharers of his culture'. [28]

Although Wilde publicly avoided Lee after the *Miss Brown* furore, her sense of an early affinity to him remained intact. When rumours of Wilde's 'illicit' conduct began to surface in 1894, Lee wrote to her mother from London that 'Oscar Wilde has got into terrible hot water' but also added that he was 'quite kind, *whatever else he may be*' (*VLL*, 380, 376; my italics). In this highly charged atmosphere, Lee published another collection of essays on Renaissance art and culture, *Renaissance Fancies and Studies*, in which she was careful to stress the growth of moral responsibility amongst the contemporary literary avant-garde. In this text, Lee bravely attempted to valorize the necessity of a morally responsible philosophy of art and life at a time when the 'tedious orthodoxy' of philistines that so disgusted Wilde appeared to have finally triumphed (Wilde, 1036). In *Renaissance Fancies and Studies*, Lee wished to assuage public anxieties about the seeming symbiosis between 'moral anarchy' and artistic innovation at present and used the example of the Renaissance to stress that the dual manifestation in contemporary culture of permissiveness and artistic experimentation was not a matter of 'cause and effect' but simply a 'coincidence' (*RFS*, 252). As part of her attempt to reorient public anxiety about the revolutionary energies of the *fin de siècle*, Lee initially acceded to the revolutionary rhetoric that surrounded the Aesthetic Movement. She argued that 'all study of past conditions and activities will eventually result, if not in the better management of the present conditions and activities ... at all events in a greater familiarity with the various kinds of character expressed in historical events and in the way of looking at them'. Lee continued that 'even if we cannot learn to guide and employ such multifold forces as make, for instance, a French revolution...we may learn to use for the best the individual minds and temperaments of those who describe them' (*RFS*, 236–7).

Renaissance Fancies and Studies includes a valedictory to Pater who had died the previous year. Despite that insistent disaffection with *The Renaissance* that drove her earlier work, Lee perceived an important precedent in Pater's career for the way in which the Aesthetic Movement could cultivate a sense of moral and social responsibility. As Lee presented it, Pater had evolved from being an 'aesthete in the very narrow sense of twenty years ago; an aesthete of the school of Mr Swinburne's' to 'a moralist' (*RFS*, 255–6). In a footnote to the essay 'Imaginative Art of the Renaissance' Lee now chose to describe Pater as a 'man whose sense of loveliness and dignity made him, *in mature life*, as learned in moral beauty as he had been in visible' (*RFS*, 114, 259; my italics). Pater's rejection of public opinion and moral convention in *The Renaissance* was now explained by Lee as not the 'contempt of the craftsman for the *bourgeois*, but [rather] the aversion of the priest for the profane uninitiated.' Under the 'solemn efficacy' of Pater's instruction, Aestheticism's new mantra, as Lee assured her reader, was now 'art, not for art's sake, but of art for the sake of life – art as one of the harmonious functions of existence' (*RFS*, 257, 259).

Both Lee's implicit sympathy with Wilde and her desire to prove to the public that aesthetes had acquired a sense of moral and social responsibility in their work and life appears to have inspired her to write the fairytale 'Prince Alberic and the Snake Lady' which appeared in the *Yellow Book* in 1896. Margaret Stetz has persuasively argued that not only the themes of the story but also Lee's dedication of it to Margaret, Lady Brooke, a friend that she and Wilde had in common, and its publication in the *Yellow Book* indicate that this fairytale was intended as an implicit tribute to the imprisoned Wilde.[29] In line with the development of Lee's responses to the high art circles that we have traced so far in both her fiction and non-fiction, alternatively, the reading of the fairytale that follows, argues that in this story Lee critiques Decadence as an artistic mode and traces the emergence of an ethical Aestheticism to supersede it. In this exquisite tale of a beautiful young aesthete who receives an education in social justice from his fairy godmother, the Snake Lady, Lee imaginatively re-conceives the Aesthetic Movement as one transformed for the wider social good. Where in *Miss Brown* Lee's reservations about the Pre-Raphaelite Movement were offset by her growing sense that high art carried within it the potential to articulate alternative and socially transformative femininities, in turn, this novella envisions the important impact that a non-normative femininity, as represented by the phallic but sexually chaste figure of the Snake Lady, could have on the Aesthetic Movement. Significantly for Lee, an ethical Aestheticism and its promised regeneration of contemporary society was, as suggested in this tale, entirely dependent upon the good offices of a woman.

Lee sets this lushly evocative tale in the fictional Italian dukedom of Luna at the turn of the eighteenth century and tells of how the ruling duke, the 'Ever Young' Balthasar Maria, pursues eternal youth, an obsession which has made him neglect his grandson and heir, Prince Alberic. The old roué lives in a Decadent castle *par excellence* and not only, as Stetz argues, does the Red Palace of Luna and its connection with the moon recall Wilde's Decadent play *Salomé* but we can also read further Decadent features in the tale in Luna's barrenness and its perverse supplanting of the natural world with artifice (Maxwell and Pulham, 121). In Lee's fictional Luna, Decadent sterility encroaches upon the animal kingdom as there are no living animals to see there but only grotesque sculptures of 'a herd of lifesize animals all carved out of various precious marbles' in a grotto in the palace. Since the prince has no access to the real beauties of Nature he has no choice but to rely upon a 'Gothic' (medieval) tapestry in his room in whose frayed borders he can see representations of 'various birds, big and little, butterflies on the lilies, snails, squirrels, mice, and rabbits'. The 'unspeakably shy and rustic' prince is so terrified by the barren Decadence of Luna that he has nightmares about his grandfather in which Balthasar Maria appears as a monstrous figure of artifice (*HAOFT*, 189, 183–5). Lee writes:

> In his green and gold wrapper and orange headdress, with the strange patches of vermilion and white on his cheeks, Duke Balthasar looked to the diseased fancy of his nephew as if he had been made of various precious metals, like the celebrated effigy he had erected of himself in the great burial-chapel' (*HAOFT*, 190)

In the boy's grotesque nightmare, not only does Balthasar embody the quintessence of the Decadent mode (make up, precious metals, and a literal morbidity) but the nightmare also conveys his subconscious realization that Decadent sterility can only bring death in its wake.

Lee's vision of art supplanting nature in this story alludes to a central theme in Wilde's writing which he had explored to highly comic effect in the essay 'The Decay of Lying' (1889). In this essay, Wilde's fictional aesthetes Vivian and Cyril favour the perfection of art and artifice over Nature's imperfections and irregularities. Wilde's principal dialogist Vivian, a 'Tired Hedonist[ ]', complains of how philistines have fixated on Nature as the absolute index of beauty and counters that 'What Art really reveals to us is Nature's lack of design, her curious crudities, her extraordinary monotony, her absolutely unfinished condition' (Wilde, 1073, 1071). Initially, Prince Alberic's obsessive examination of Nature through an artistic representation in the tapestry appears to suggest that he will grow up to be an Aesthete in the Wildean mould. Lee remarks that the tapestry makes Alberic 'look forward to seeing the real things only when he should be grown up' which implicitly signals that to her the Wildean aesthete's love of art and artifice over Nature represents a juvenile state of mind (*HAOFT*, 185). And here we are also reminded of the aesthetes' refusal in *Miss Brown* to allow Hamlin to 'revolutionise poetry' by a return to Nature as its subject matter.

While Decadence fills the boy with terror and horror, an alternative reality is offered to him by the tapestry. As Alberic grows older he can make out a picture at the centre of the tapestry which features his ancestor, the first Prince Alberic and his meeting with the Snake Lady. As legend has it, the Snake Lady, Oriana, is a beautiful fairy who has been cursed to take the shape of a snake, except for one hour at sunset, until a Prince Alberic of the House of Luna fulfils a ten-year vow of chastity and so can release her. Alberic grows up to be a beautiful young man whose 'figure was at once manly and delicate' and whose hair significantly 'seemed to imply almost a woman's care and coquetry'. Where his effeminate appearance references the beautiful and delicate aesthetes of Wilde's dialogues and fiction, Alberic's decision to undertake the vow of chastity and allow himself to be educated by his 'dear Godmother' suggests a sexual and ethical regeneration of aestheticism (*HAOFT*, 198, 202). Unlike his grandfather, Alberic is chaste and he seeks to reform financial mismanagement of Luna.

The Snake Lady is also a figure who in the *fin-de-siècle* context is replete with many meanings. While Oriana challenges those immemorial visions of female evil – from Eve to Medusa – that abound in Western culture, her wish that Alberic should remain chaste while she undertakes his education in social responsibility allows Lee to envisage the ethical transformation of (masculine) aestheticism at a woman's hands. Additionally, the Snake Lady is a phallic figure and, by extension, Oriana can be seen to represent a type of masculine woman. When allied, in the final instance, to her commitment to reforming male sexuality, the character of Oriana suggests itself as Lee's imaginative presentation of that *fin-de-siècle* feminist, the New Woman. Lee uses the Herculean tasks traditionally demanded of heroes and heroines in fairytales as a figure for the social purity campaigns of late-Victorian feminists. Indeed, Oriana's insistence upon Alberic's chastity recalls one of the main tenets of late-Victorian feminism. Sally Ledger writes that at the end of the Victorian period:

> Feminists were concerned less with female sexuality than with male sexuality, which they condemned as an oppressive pollutant of society. The general drift of the social purity movement was such that men were being asked to match the 'high standards' of sexual purity and chastity that had so long been enforced on women[.][30]

Having transcended both his grandfather's Decadent world and his own youthful (Wildean) aestheticism, Alberic comes to embody the kind of ethical aestheticism that Lee propounded in *Renaissance Fancies and Studies*: 'art not for art's sake, but as one of the harmonious functions of existence' (*RFS*, 259). In many ways, we can see that Wilde's imprisonment, in essence his punishment for his sexual difference, is used by Lee as a platform from which she began to articulate in the highly encoded form of the fairytale her own progressive vision of the social transformation and positive benefits to society that the non-normative sexualities of the masculine woman and effeminate man could bring about. And yet, the murder of Oriana and the early death of Alberic that this causes, suggests that in 1896 Lee realized that contemporary society was unwilling to channel the potential of such exceptional men and women. One virulent opponent of the New Woman, the Rev. W. F. Barry, prophesied in an article for the *Quarterly Review* that the 'masculine' New Woman's attempt to enter the traditionally male preserve of politics, athletics and medicine would only rebound upon her. This commentator portentously observed that:

> Woman, in spite of athletics, universal suffrage, and clinical lectures, is not likely to be transformed into man. She may become abnormal, but the ape of the masculine remains what she was, her beauty gone, her least desirable qualities heightened, by the detestable male habits which she has been ridiculous enough to assume. [31]

Given her own sexually indeterminate identity, we can only imagine the disquiet that such widely held intransigence must have caused Lee.

2

Experiments in Short Fiction

Vernon Lee published more than twenty short stories and novellas during her career. Her first short story to appear in print, 'Les aventures d'une pièce de monnaie' (1869), was published serially in the French journal *La famille* when she was thirteen and her last collection of 'fantastic' tales, which she wrote for her friend Maurice Baring, came out in 1927. It is evident that Lee was consistently attracted to the short story form from the fact that she returned to the genre over and again whilst continuing to produce various works of cultural history, aesthetics and psychology. As we saw in the previous chapter with the example of 'Prince Alberic and the Snake Lady', in many ways, Lee used her short fiction to offer a more personalized and less guarded imaginative articulation of ideas that she was simultaneously developing in her non-fiction writing. In her meditation on the craft of writing, *The Handling of Words*, Lee praised the short story form for the concentrated expression of an idea that it allowed and, in this, compared it to 'a poem or little play' (*HW*, 19). And clearly, as can be seen in her stories' powerful evocation of the 'genius loci' of the places that she had visited and in her imaginary portraits which palpably bring to life historical characters, Lee's short fiction fully exploits the genre's capacity for intensity and economy of effect.

The continental settings of much of Lee's short fiction also suggest a significant link between her expatriate identity and her use of the short story form. Here, Hilary Fraser's recent account of Lee's national identity as one that was simultaneously dislocated *and* productively cosmopolitan can be helpfully extended to explore the ways in which Lee's interstitial national identity came to shape her short fiction.[1] In the readings that follow, we examine how in the tale 'Amour Dure' (1887, 1890) a

Polish scholar suffers from an agonized sense of his own cultural marginalization in Italy; later, the novella 'Lady Tal' (1892) reveals Lee's formal interest in 'in-between' literary spaces as the story critiques popular fiction from a high art perspective and *vice versa*. And finally, the choices Lee made in 'The Virgin of the Seven Daggers' (1896, 1902, 1927) in terms of the original language of its composition (French), her subsequent translation of the story into English and her response to continental literary forms are, as we will see, born of a further creative disjunction between English letters and European 'high art'. As will become increasingly apparent from this chapter, to Lee Europe and European culture were both a source of creative inspiration and the cause of much ethical and emotional anxiety.

While much of Lee's fiction and non-fictional works of cultural history and travel-writing attempt to convey the genius loci of the numerous places that she had visited on the continent, undoubtedly, her most ardent attachment was to her designated homeland, Italy. Vineta Colby's explanation that in Italy Lee found 'a combination more natural, more aesthetically pleasing, and more spiritually satisfying' than anywhere else is confirmed by Lee's pensive and wistful soliloquizing in *The Tower of the Mirrors and Other Essays on the Spirit of Places* (1914) in which she asked herself whether she 'Had...ever really cared for any country except Italy?' (Colby, 256, 259). Given her strength of feeling for Italy, it is surprising to discover that Lee found the presiding spirit of her adopted homeland was not one that afforded an easy spiritual sympathy, but rather one that produced a peculiarly disquieting frisson in the mind. In another passage from *The Tower of the Mirrors*, Lee wrote of how Italy engendered a visceral response that threatened to overwhelm her. Stopping to look at frescoes at Castiglione d'Ologna she is moved to ask:

> Why is Italy full of such places? Why is its past not homely and warm and close to us like that of the North [Europe] but distant, forlorn, tragic with the smell of dead leaves and of charnel, with its gaunt show of splendour crumbling in base uses: a past whereof one fails to understand the real reasons for greatness, and oftener still the reasons for decay? (quoted in Colby, 258).

Lee had begun her attempt to understand and explain the speedy cultural evolution of Italy in the Renaissance period and its subsequent 'decay' some thirty years earlier in *Euphorion* (1884), her first cultural history of the Renaissance. While Lee opened this study by declaring her allegiance to the impressionist method, ironically, it was her personal intimacy with Italy and her desire to remain faithful to it that threatened to undermine the avowedly impressionist remit of the introduction. From the first essay onwards, Lee's writing on the Italian Renaissance indicates a decidedly less idealistic and more pragmatic response to the subject than that found in the work of fellow cultural historians J. A. Symonds and Walter Pater. For example, where in *The Renaissance, Studies in Art and Poetry,* Pater wrote that 'a spirit of general elevation and enlightenment' characterized the period, Lee was less sanguine and adulatory about the age (Pater, xxxiii). Renaissance Italy to her was a 'loathsome mixture of good and evil' that saw '[the Italian] people moving on towards civilization and towards chaos' (*E*, 1:15, 1: 29). While she agreed with Pater and Symonds that the period led people to cast off feudalism and 'the morbid, monastic ways of feeling' equally, she argues that this new social freedom brought with it a dangerous permissiveness. Lee regretfully informed the reader that in this period 'humanists inoculated literature with the filthiest refuse cast up by antiquity; nay, even civic and family ties were loosened; assassinations and fratricides began to abound, and all law, human and divine, to be set at defiance' (*E*, 1:29). Ultimately, Lee felt that by spearheading the Renaissance in Europe the Italian nation had paid a great price. '[I]n short,' she wrote 'while the morality of the Italians was sacrificed to obtain the knowledge on which modern society depends, the political existence of Italy was sacrificed to the diffusion of that knowledge, and that the nation was not only doomed to immorality, but doomed also to the inability to reform' (*E*, 1: 53– 4).

In presenting both the good and evil sides of the Italian Renaissance to the modern reader, Lee sought to forestall the trend in modern histories that glamorized the Italian Renaissance without giving an objective view of the moral shortcomings of the period. As noted earlier, Lee gave a pointed warning against the 'Dramatic emotion...[the] egotistic...[and]

half-artistic pleasure' which was becoming the mainstay of modern historical scholarship and that the history of the Renaissance, in particular, 'has been made to pander but too much'. Here, 'egotistic' stands as a particularly damning criticism of the impressionist method as Lee suggested that it was pure narcissism to believe that the modern mind could fully comprehend preceding cultures and was adamant that '[t]he moral atmosphere of those days...[is] as impossible for us to breathe as would be the physical atmosphere of the moon'. As we can see, for Lee, moral relativism did not promise a heightened empathy with the historical object but rather left the reader vulnerable to the alien and pernicious atmosphere of the past. It would seem that as much as Lee was attracted to, and deployed, the impressionist historical method, she felt that its attempts to erase historical difference posed a dangerous threat to the moral equanimity and enlightened mores of the modern reader. 'Out of the Renaissance, out of the Middle Ages,' Lee pronounced, 'we must never hope to evoke any spectres which can talk with us and we with them' (E, 1:12–13, 1:22).

RENAISSANCE SPECTRES: 'AMOUR DURE'

While in *Euphorion* Lee counselled a strict policing of the historical divide that separated the Renaissance from the nineteenth century, she was to take up an entirely different position in relation to the imaginative fiction that she wrote. In her preface to her collection of four supernatural tales, *Hauntimgs: Fantastic Stories* (1890), Lee presents her fictional ghosts as ones that have 'haunted certain brains, and have haunted, among others, my own and my friends' (*HAOFT*, 40). Indeed, in this collection of four supernatural tales ('Amour Dure: Passages from the Diary of Spiridion Trepka', 'Dionea', 'Oke of Okehurst; Or, the Phantom Lover' and 'A Wicked Voice') Lee uses her apparent possession by her psychological ghosts to license visceral and feverish critiques of prevalent trends in contemporary 'high' culture that are of quite a different order to those found in her numerous essays on cultural history. For example, as seen in the previous chapter, one way in which we can read one of the tales of the collection,

'Oke of Okehurst' (a reprint of *A Phantom Lover*) is as a dramatic rendition of Lee's acute anxieties over the moral danger courted by aesthetes in their fervent devotion to Pater's aesthetic philosophy. Another of the stories from this collection, 'Amour Dure', dramatizes the possession of the mind of a modern scholar by the Italy of the Renaissance period. This story both powerfully conveys the historical frisson that Lee felt from Italy and what she described as the overmastering power of its past. As a tale of madness induced by unguarded historical enquiry, 'Amour Dure' can also be read as a highly-coloured dramatization of the concerns that Lee expressed in *Euphorion* on the temptations and insidious moral dangers posed to the modern mind by the impressionist historical method.

The tale is told through the diary entries of a young Polish historian, Spiridion Trepka, who, on a research trip to the fictional Italian town of Urbania, becomes obsessed by the history of an aristocratic woman from the Renaissance period, Medea da Carpi. While she had been reduced in modern times to a wicked witch in children's fairytales, the historical Medea was renowned as a dangerous beauty who used her attractions to seize control of Urbania, was implicated in numerous love affairs and murders, and was secretly executed by Urbania's rightful ruler, Duke Robert, in 1585. Having read the accounts of Medea written by male Renaissance chroniclers, Trepka's sympathies initially lie with Duke Robert but the chance discovery of Medea's portrait in the town's historical archive leads him to revise his judgement. Isolated and in thrall to Medea's beauty, Trepka abandons all scholarly restraint and objective method to reconstruct her life based on his impressions of her portrait. Ironically, through his archival research, Trepka indulges in precisely the kind of moral relativism that Lee warned against in *Euphorion*. Trepka imbibes the atmosphere of the Renaissance and seeks not only to understand Medea in the context of the Machiavellian machinations of a Renaissance court but also comes to explain her black reputation for murder as crimes necessary to her survival. His desire to understand her debilitates into a state of pathological empathy that leads him to believe that the long-dead woman has made contact with him. For Lee, it seems that the end-product of the impressionist historical mode and its attempt to enter into a communion with Renaissance personalities can only bring hysteria and insanity in its wake. However, the conclusion of the tale undermines the reader's assumption that the historian's contact with Medea has been no more than an elaborate fantasy, as the morning after Trepka's longed-for meeting with Medea, a newspaper reports that the Professor has been found stabbed to death. Whether imagined or not, this is another assignation with the Renaissance *femme fatale* which ends, as all encounters with her have done, in the death of the unfortunate lover.

Like another tale in the *Hauntings* collection, 'A Wicked Voice', 'Amour Dure' links the purported supernatural encounter to the protagonist's disturbed sense of his own national and cultural dislocation. From the outset, Lee indicates that Trepka's uncanny experience is born from his sense of himself as a disenfranchised colonial (Polish) subject of the German empire.[2] 'Amour Dure' opens with Trepka voicing his disdain for the German historians he met in Rome. To him they are 'Berlin and Munich Vandals'; he fears that his scholarship has been compromised by having accepted a research grant from the German government and wonders whether this makes him complicit in the pillaging of Italian culture, of which he accuses German historians. 'Am I not myself a product of modern, northern civilisation;' Trepka asks himself 'is not my coming to Italy due to this very modern scientific vandalism, which has given me a travelling scholarship because I have written a book like all those other atrocious books of erudition and art-criticism?' Trepka feels that the whole apparatus of contemporary German scholarship is bent on obscuring any authentic insight into Renaissance Italy he might have. He anxiously describes himself as 'a Pole grown into the semblance of a German pedant' and worries that the whole paraphernalia of the professional academic acts as a hindrance to him 'ever com[ing] in spirit into the presence of the Past'. Thus Trepka believes himself to be doubly colonised both by Germany through its control of his homeland and what he perceives to be a parallel annexing of his scholarship (*HAOFT*, 41–2).

Lee emphasizes how Trepka's anxiety at his colonized status is central to the tragic unravelling of his mind that follows. Catherine Maxwell and Patricia Pulham's recent description of Medea as a 'sixteenth-century political intriguer' and of the 'revisionary history' that Trepka wishes to write of her is suggestive ('Introduction', *HAOFT*, 12). By extension, we might read Trepka's decision to abandon the history of Urbania that he is being paid to write by the German government as an implicit act of political resistance, on his part, inspired by Medea, both against German academic orthodoxy and German political hegemony more widely. His revolt against German pedantry leads Trepka to believe that he will only discover the authentic spirit of Italy's past through an imaginative engagement with it. On entering Urbania, Trepka describes the powerful feelings that the town summons up. He tells how he half expects to see a 'troop of horsemen, with beaked helmets and clawed shoes...emerge, with armour glittering and pennons waving in the sunset'. Given Trepka's anxieties about the annexing of his scholarship, his homeland and Italy's past by Germans and Germany that preface this scene, this imagined scenario of Renaissance soldiers readying themselves for battle that he conjures up appears to externalize his desire to resist his own colonized status. The strength of his passionate apostrophizing that the horsemen scene 'was Italy, it was the Past!' evokes the kinds of warnings that Lee had given in *Euphorion* against the 'egotistic' 'dramatic' and 'half-artistic' pleasures of the impressionist mode (*HAOFT*, 42). In this tale, Trepka appears not to have come into genuine contact with the 'genius locus' of Italy but, as Lee had warned in her study of the Italian Renaissance, seems only to be in a narcissistic and dangerous communion with his own impressions.

Initially, Trepka's empathy for Medea might also appear to be the product of the comparatively more enlightened sexual politics of the nineteenth century. In the Urbanian archive, Trepka speculates on the nature of the marriage that Medea was forced into at the age of fourteen. Here, Lee emphasizes that it is not an enlightened modern sensibility that underpins Trepka's justification of Medea's involvement in murder and treachery but his total acquiescence to the immorality of the Renaissance period. He persuades himself to 'put aside all pedantic modern ideas of right and wrong' because he believes that 'in a century of violence and treachery' no such moral absolutes can be applied. Trepka's slide into what Lee had described in *Euphorion* as a pernicious moral relativism leads him to compare Medea approvingly to another infamous Renaissance woman, the real-life historical figure of Lucrezia Borgia, aristocrat and incestuous poisoner. He celebrates such Renaissance women not only for their 'extreme distinction of beauty' but also for their 'terribleness of nature'.[3] Lee also shows how Trepka's impressionist method is intimately connected to his desire for Medea. On seeing her portrait for the first time he is struck by her 'curious, at first rather conventional, artificial-looking sort of beauty, voluptuous yet cold,' and he 'often examine[s] these tragic portraits, wondering what this face, which led so many men to their death, may have been like when it spoke or smiled, what at the moment when Medea da Carpi fascinated her victims into love unto death'. Trepka's absorption with the past and this dangerous beauty is so complete that he believes that it would be impossible to find such a *femme fatale* to love amongst modern women (*HAOFT*, 54–6, 52).

Christa Zorn has read the story as Lee's direct response to Walter Pater's impressionist criticism and, in particular, his reading of another iconic and troubling real-life Renaissance beauty: *The Mona Lisa*. Zorn persuasively argues that Trepka's sympathetic understanding of the reality of Medea's life can be interpreted as Lee's reversal 'of [Pater's] mythmaking' to 'let us see the mind behind it' (Zorn, 158). That Lee offers further challenges to Pater's reading of *The Mona Lisa* is also evident from the difference in symbolic meaning and affect that Lee chooses to accord her own portrait of a Renaissance *femme fatale*. In the previous chapter we saw how in her first reprisal of *The Mona Lisa* trope in *A Phantom Lover*, Lee critiqued Pater's reading of the Da Vinci painting. However provocative and morally hazardous Pater's prose-poem might have been, ultimately for Lee, his rendering of *La Gioconda* as a passive embodiment of masculine desire invalidated his attempt to figure the portrait as a symbol of a progressive sexual and social order. In the denouement of the tale, Alice Oke's rebellious attempts to transcend the passivity that she has been ascribed as a modern-day Lady Lisa end in tragedy.

We see Lee explore Pater's reading of *The Mona Lisa* from another angle in 'Amour Dure'. In his disquieting reading of Da Vinci's portrait, Pater had implied that 'evil' had a progressive role to play in the development of modern European civilization.

Thus, Pater read *The Mona Lisa* as an embodiment of 'the animalism of Greece, the lust of Rome ... [and] the sins of the Borgias'. He also envisioned the portrait as the figurehead of a progressively modern and permissive philosophy which embraced the cyclical nature and connectivity of *all* human experience, however morally disturbing the modern reader might find it. To Pater, *The Mona Lisa* both represented the 'fancy of a perpetual life, sweeping together ten thousand experiences' and also 'modern philosophy['s]' conception of 'the idea of humanity as wrought upon by, and summing up in itself, all modes of thought and life' (Pater, 80). In comparison to Pater's highly influential reading of the Da Vinci painting, the resurrection of Lee's Medea promises nothing productive or progressive for the development of the modern mind as, even beyond the grave, Medea continues to exhort men to desperate acts of self-immolation. In Trepka's demise, we see how an unguarded yoking of the Renaissance and the modern mind together was certainly anathema to Lee. And, in this, her second reprisal of the *Mona Lisa* trope, Lee shows that she remained entirely pessimistic about the dangers posed to the modern mind by scholarly celebrations of Renaissance immorality.

ARTISTS, TRADESMEN AND THE LITERARY MARKETPLACE: 'LADY TAL'

In a letter that she wrote to her brother in 1893, while she complained of her lack of popular success, Lee was equally pragmatic about the kinds of pressures that popular success might have exerted on her development as a professional writer. She tells Eugene:

> Of course I have played my cards as badly as I could have done with regards to securing a public; but I have written, for the last ten years with the determination *never* to write a thing which did not happen to interest me at the moment, and with the desire to prevent myself from getting into intellectual ruts.

> At thirty seven I have no public, but on the other hand, I am singularly far from being played out and crystallised, as I see most writers become even before this age (*VLL*, 364; emphasis in original).

And yet Lee's avowed decision not to pursue popular success is belied by the fact that between 1886 and 1896, a decade that saw both the final demise of the three-decker Victorian novel and an attendant growth of a new and buoyant market for short fiction, Lee's fictional output was entirely confined to the short story.[4] Retrospectively, two writer friends of Lee's, Henry James and H. G. Wells, gave quite different opinions on the heightened attention that the genre received in this period. For James, the advent of the high art bible the *Yellow Book* was particularly important in the development of the genre for allowing it to 'assume' and 'shamelessly parade in, its own organic form'.[5] Conversely for H. G. Wells, the short story was no denizen of the Decadent coterie but rather had accrued a more democratic appeal by the end of the century. Wells judged the 1890s to be 'a good and stimulating period for a short-story writer' and remembered the infectious enthusiasm for the form on the part of both readers and writers in the final decade of the Victorian period. Wells declared that 'People talked about [short stories]... tremendously, compared them, and ranked them. That was the thing that mattered'.[6] Given Wells's comments about the popularity of short fiction at the *fin de siècle*, Lee's disavowal to her brother of any desire for popular renown appears not only a little disingenuous but also points to a characteristic tension that we can recognize in her short stories between the popularity of the form and the rarefied and often self–reflexive subject-matter of her tales. In the reading of the novella 'Lady Tal' that follows, we shall see how Lee not only humorously deploys the tensions between highbrow literature and popular fiction, more generally, for comic effect but also positions her personal anxieties about the reception of her own work in the context of a topical *fin-de-siècle* debate over whether highbrow literature could ultimately survive in a market flooded with popular fiction.

In 1892, Lee took her imaginative fiction in an entirely new and surprising direction with the publication of three novellas ('Lady Tal', 'A Worldly Woman' and 'The Legend of Madame Krasinska') under the heading *Vanitas: Polite Stories*. With this collection, Lee promised to turn her acute intelligence upon the subject of the exigencies and the waste of human energy demanded by fashionable life and, in particular, the psychological damage caused to middle and upper-class women by the stultifying conditions imposed by a decorative life. Given Lee's formidable intellectual reputation, her appeal in the preface to *Vanitas* for the existential significance of the experiences of the most 'frivolous' of society women that she had dramatised in this collection is certainly unexpected. In the introduction to the collection, Lee is emphatic in her justification of her decision to fictionalise such an uncharacteristically 'trivial' subject and insists that 'round these sketches of frivolous women, there have gathered some of the least frivolous thoughts, heaven knows, that have ever come into my head'. For Lee, while her reader might see no value in such lives, she, herself, believes that 'the great waste of precious things, delicate discernment, quick feeling and sometimes stoical fortitude, involved in frivolous life' should invoke our pity as such a 'creature', according to her, sadly has 'little inkling of the sense of brotherhood and duty which changes one, from a blind dweller in caves, to an inmate of the real world of storms and sunshine' (*V*, v–vi).

If, as the introduction to *Vanitas* seemed to promise, readers expected to find a dramatic exposition of the political and ethical implications of the unproductive lives that middle and upper-class women were forced to live, they would have been disappointed. Indeed, it would not be until 1902 that Lee fully conceptualized and articulated her understanding of the question of women's so-called 'sex-parasitism'. In 'The Economic Dependence of Women', her review essay of the American feminist Charlotte Perkins Gilman's pioneering work *Women and Economics* (1898), Lee sought to understand the financial value of women's labour from both a political and ethical standpoint. Where Gilman understood economic and political individualism to foster social networks, conversely, Lee argued that women 'worked not for the consumption of the world at large, and subject to the world's selection of good or bad, useful or useless work; but for the consumption of one man and subject to that one man's preferences'. For Lee, first and foremost, the outcome of this male 'greed' was the unethical basis on which it founded society. '[W]ithin the community a system of units of virtuous egoism, a network of virtuous rapacity', Lee wrote, '... has made the supposed organic social whole a mere gigantic delusion' (*GA*, 279, 287). In 1902, it seems that Lee's sexual politics took a radically separatist turn.

Curiously, the first story of *Vanitas*, the comic tale 'Lady Tal', appears to immediately undermine the earnest commitment that Lee made in the preface to understanding the waste of human energies required to maintain a frivolous life. Given her anxieties about the reception of her work and her lack of popular success, this tale of a philistine aristocrat, the eponymous Lady Tal, who writes an execrable novel about the suffering of a society woman in order to make 'pots of money' and gain financial independence for herself appears to be both flippantly self-reflexive and self-satirizing in tenor (*V*, 49). (And here, we cannot help but wonder if Lee was trying to make light of some personal trepidation that she might have felt about how the particular change in direction of her work that *Vanitas* signalled might be received.) Lady Tal cajoles a successful American novelist of the school of Henry James, Jervase Marion, to read her novel for her. In turn, he becomes interested in Lady Tal from a purely psychological point of view and cannot stop himself, try as he might, from thinking of her as a character for a new novel. Here, it is tempting to read Marion's private reflections about Lady Tal's novel ('The story was no story at all, merely the unnoticed martyrdom of a delicate and scrupulous woman' (*V*, 44)), as an implicit acknowledgement on Lee's part of how incongruous the seemingly 'insubstantial' feminine subject-matter of *Vanitas* would appear, when compared either to the polemical force of *Miss Brown* or the demonstrably more 'masculine' intellectual concerns of her non-fiction work.

In 'Lady Tal' Lee demonstrates, for the first time, her aptitude for comic writing by crafting a breezily jocular satire about Henry James and the Jamesian narrative method. As with many of Lee's professional relationships to celebrated male writers such as J. A. Symonds, Walter Pater and Oscar Wilde her association with James was somewhat fraught. As noted in the previous chapter much to James's embarrassment, Lee had dedicated *Miss Brown* to him. While undoubtedly, it would be erroneous to read 'Lady Tal' as a delayed rejoinder on Lee's part to James, nonetheless, unflattering resemblances between the real Henry James and the character of Jervase Marion are

49

difficult to ignore. They range from the crudely comic device of Marion wearing boots that are too tight for him (as James reportedly did) to the description of Marion as 'a dainty but frugal bachelor' with well-modulated speech (*V*, 12; Colby, 193). Moreover, the *mise-en-scène* of the tale has recognizably Jamesian inflections since its portrait of a gossipy ex-pat society in Italy, financial intrigue amongst the leisured classes and the seemingly eccentric behaviour of a rich young woman all call to mind James's novel *The Portrait of a Lady*.

Marion's almost pathological desire to discover the truth of Lady Tal's history in order to turn it into fiction also mirrors the advice that the real Henry James had given to Lee, in the aftermath of the publication of *Miss Brown*, in improving her skills as a novelist. Lee recalls in a letter to Maurice Baring how James had told her that 'his plan through life has been never to lose an opportunity of seeing anything of any kind; he urges me to do the same' (quoted in Colby, 109). However, in 'Lady Tal' the insight into the human condition, that following the Jamesian method promises to elicit, induces nothing but guilt and acute anxiety in Marion. While to the outside observer, Marion appears to be 'the dispassionate spectator of the world's follies and miseries' in his own private reflections, he fears that the cultivation of such disinterest on his part verges on mania because he cannot seem to stop his 'hateful habit of studying people, of turning them round, prodding and cutting them to see what was inside' (*V*, 53, 47). Ironically, in Lee's story Marion is worsted by his own psychological interrogation of Lady Tal, as it turns out that she has allowed him to think that he can use her as the subject of his new novel in order to coerce him into helping her write her novel 'Christina'. In Lee's tale the Jamesian method rebounds on its proponent to broadly comic effect. We might even speculate that Lady Tal's decision to dedicate her novel to Marion and his evident discomfort at this might have been Lee's mischievous scripting into the story of Henry James's acute embarrassment at having *Miss Brown* dedicated to him.

Lady Tal's life-story suggests itself to Jervase Marion as perfect material from which he might craft his next novel. She is the beautiful widow of a fabulously wealthy but miserly husband, the terms of whose will forbid her from remarrying and Marion is also fascinated by her devotion to her invalid brother who died an early death. Lady Tal's refusal to fade into a decorous mourning has led Venetian society to judge her to have insulted her brother's memory, and it also believes that the fall-out from her terrible marriage has unleashed a dangerous and reckless independence in her. Marion muses on the new novel that he will write in which Lady Tal will feature as the central protagonist:

> Lady Tal (Marion couldn't fix on a name for her) would gradually be sucked back into frivolous and futile and heartless society; the *hic* of the whole story being the slow ebbing of that noble influence, the daily encroachments of the baser sides of Lady Tal's own nature, and of the base side of the world (*V*, 87).

And yet, Lady Tal's bluff aristocratic manner entirely upends the Jamesian script in which Marion wishes to place her. Rather comically, the 'sensitive' novelist finds himself to be a little frightened of her and he is disconcerted to find that she invokes in him 'a vague repulsion due to her dreadful strength'. Her conscious assumption of a 'quiet, aggressive...inscrutability' begins to undermine Marion's belief in his own perceptiveness (*V*, 36, 57).

In the previous chapter we saw how in *Miss Brown* and *A Phantom Lover* the fictional male Pre-Raphaelite and Aesthetic artist is ultimately revealed as having no interest in understanding his female subject. Lee emphasizes that the artistic reputation of both men is essentially dependent upon fixing Miss Brown or Mrs Oke in the iconic 'high art' mould of the enigmatic and inscrutable woman. By comparison, in 'Lady Tal' Lee subtly reverses this power dynamic by presenting the female subject consciously taking on the veneer of impenetrability in order to overmaster and outwit the mentoring male artist. Lady Tal is fully aware that Marion wishes to use her as a psychological case study for his new novel and she manipulates his 'hateful habit of studying people' by consciously remaining an enigma in order to ensnare and compel him, against his better judgement, into helping her with the novel that she is writing (*V*, 47). Playfully in 'Lady Tal', not only does the female popular novelist deflate the artistic conceit of the 'highbrow' male artist but she also reveals his vulnerability to his own

51

artistic method. Moreover, the kind of popular fiction that Lady Tal hopes to write means that her coercing of Marion into a professional association with her also threatens his artistic integrity. Figuratively in this novella, highbrow literature, as represented by Marion, is seen to be vulnerable to the encroachments of popular fiction.

And yet equally, Lee critiques popular fiction from the high art perspective. Marion finds the novel that Lady Tal is writing, 'Christina', to be entirely derivative whilst her syntax, grammar and mode of expression are even more inadequate. Even though the work has no conceivable literary merit, Lady Tal is convinced that she will become, as she incongruously puts it, the 'New George Eliot of fashionable life'. With no thought for artistic merit or the rules of composition, she carelessly speculates before Marion, the successful novelist, that 'one makes pots of money in your business, doesn't one?' (*V*, 100, 49).

Lady Tal's novel also functions as a device which allows Lee to participate in a topical *fin-de-siècle* debate about the kinds of pressures that artists faced from the literary marketplace. According to the critic Nigel Cross, the period between 1880 and 1895 saw a significant shift in terms of the writing of creative fiction. Cross writes that in this period 'Literature, especially fiction, became a battleground between "tradesmen" as [George] Gissing called them, writers such as Walter Besant, Anthony Hope, and Andrew Lang, and "artists" such as Henry James, George Meredith and Gissing himself, who had little confidence in the market-place but some confidence in posterity'.[7] In his novel *New Grub Street*, Gissing produced a pessimistic tale about the triumph of writers who approached writing as a trade and literature as a commodity over 'true' artists. Gissing's novel is a Darwinian tale in which those who treat art as a trade survive and thrive while artists who 'refuse to be of one's time...[face] breakdown and wretchedness'.[8] As seen in Lee's letter to her brother of the following year, her lack of popular success made her conceive of her writing as a vocation rather than a profitable trade. In 'Lady Tal', the 'artist' and 'tradesmen' debate is turned into a comic farce as Lee's two protagonists play out the Darwinian struggle between the artist (Marion) and the tradesman (Lady Tal) as slapstick. On being bullied into carrying Lady Tal's shopping, Marion experiences 'acute physical discomfort [and]...[i]t seemed as if this terrible, aristocratic giantess were doing it all on purpose to make him miserable. He saw that he was intensely ridiculous in her eyes' (*V*, 63). The comic tale finishes with Lady Tal's revelation that they have both been using each other all along. The reader is surprised to find that, despite her aristocratic bluntness, it is Lady Tal who has subtly manipulated Marion throughout. The hypersensitive male artist's belief in his privileged knowledge of his subject is lightly satirized as supercilious and easily manipulated. And in Lady Tal's final suggestion that Marion might do better artistically and financially by seeking her input on *his* next novel, the ending of the story teasingly leaves unresolved the contemporary debate about whether it is the artist or tradesman who will ultimately triumph in the literary marketplace.

While the novella is unique in Lee's oeuvre for not ending in disaster and tragedy, it was not unique in the personal costs it extorted. As *Miss Brown* had offended Wilde and others, 'Lady Tal', unsurprisingly, cost Lee her friendship with James. Although James did not read the tale, report of it was enough for him to tell his brother William that the piece was a 'particularly imprudent & blackguardly sort of thing to do to a friend & one who has treated her with such particular consideration as I have'. Years later, Lee complained to her friend Maurice Baring that she thought James had been oversensitive in his response. 'I have myself put a full-length description of Henry James into a story', she wrote, 'but as, although it was funny, it was also kind and respectful, and I considered...H. J.'s years of resentment as very absurd and unjust' (quoted in Colby, 196–7).

As witty as the story 'Lady Tal' is, its presence as the opening story of the collection *Vanitas* destabilizes both the avowed sincerity of the preface and the overt commitment to exploring the experience of 'frivolous' women that we see in the two stories that follow. 'A Worldly Woman' is a tale in which a young upper-class woman, Val Flodden, asks a poor artist to educate her. To the artist, Val 'was the living example of the ignorance of all higher right and wrong, of all the larger facts of existence, in which the so-called upper classes lived on no better than heathen blacks'. His vaguely 'socialistic' prejudices against the upper classes lead him to refuse to help her (*V*, 157–8, 197). (Significantly, in one scene the characters have a heated discussion about the merits of Henry James's novel *Princess Casamassima* (1885–6) and disagree over whether the princess's commitment to socialism is mere enthusiasm (*V*, 189–92)). They meet again a decade later when Val is now a disappointed and dissipated society hostess. Lee highlights the compromises that high society demands of women, in which they are forced to abandon both the possibility of a vocation and the potential for doing good in society in exchange for financial security. Val's unavoidable economic dependence (and here, the modern reader will undoubtedly find Lee's casual slip into anti-Semitism distasteful) has led her to marry 'an odd sample of Jewry acclimatised in England, a horrid, half-handsome man, with extraordinarily bland manners and an extraordinarily hard expression, obstinate and mocking' (*V*, 206). In the third tale of *Vanitas*, 'The Legend of Madame Krasinska', Lee gives a portrait of the eponymous society hostess who has nothing better to do than heedlessly dress up as an insane pauper woman for a costume ball. Madame Krasinska's callousness rebounds on her and she finds that she so intensely identifies with the beggar that it brings her to the point of suicide.

In writing three novellas that all ostensibly dramatize the misery of women in high society, the collection bridges the psychological fiction of Henry James – as suggested earlier, *The Portrait of a Lady* is an important intertext for 'Lady Tal' – and the work of women Modernist writers of the next generation such as Virginia Woolf and Katherine Mansfield. James's Isabel Archer is duped into giving up her lively sense of personal freedom in her marriage to the unsavoury American Aesthete Gilbert Osmond. Later, Woolf and Mansfield would, themselves, take up unfulfilled society women as their subjects in a short story such as 'Bliss' (1920) and a novel such as *Mrs Dalloway* (1925). Like Lee before them, both Mansfield and Woolf in 'Bliss' and *Mrs Dalloway* respectively, would use the domestic setting and the occasion of a party to bring their fictional society women to a moment of self-awareness about the ultimate futility of such a life. And yet, Lee's decision to preface two stories that apparently sincerely invite sympathy for 'frivolous' women with a satire about the writing of such fiction is essentially inconsistent. Ultimately, it is difficult to decide whether Lee's strategy for *Vanitas* was to playfully satirize the unexpected change in direction of her literary output or whether the contradictions of this collection seriously convey a continued anxiety on Lee's part about the particular reception of her own writing and women's writing *per se*.

BOWDLERIZED BAUDELAIRE: 'THE VIRGIN OF THE SEVEN DAGGERS'

The final tale examined in this chapter is 'The Virgin of the Seven Daggers'. Unquestionably the most cosmopolitan and complex of Lee's short fiction, this tale brings together and extends in a new direction the unsettling European cultural encounters which had variously characterized the *Hauntings* collection. As we shall see, this darkly comic tale not only reveals, for the first time, anxieties on Lee's part about her own identity as a cultured and cosmopolitan European critic, but also appears to anticipate the metafictional techniques most closely associated with postmodern fiction. Over its three extant versions – one which Lee wrote in French in 1896, its English translation of 1902 and a final English version of 1926 which included a preface explaining the genesis of the tale – we see seventeenth-century Catholic Spain confront the Moorish past that it has denied and Lee 'the puritan aesthete' respond to the less than salubrious work of the nineteenth-century French poet Charles Baudelaire. In the final version, we see a new preface offset the apparently pernicious cosmopolitan inflections of the tale with the sanguine and familiar comforts of a Victorian country-house.[9] Formally, Lee also experiments with different literary registers in the story by offering a parody of Baudelairean Decadence and incongruously yoking it to her childhood reading of an expurgated edition of the Orientalist fantasy *Arabian Nights* before ending by mischievously offering the whole tale to her newly-converted Catholic friend Maurice Baring as a mildly anti-Catholic satire. However, the ending of this hybrid tale does not offer a final resolution as Lee chooses to close the story by blurring the line between fact and fiction, artistic authority and irreverent pastiche in order to pose further questions about the nature of literary authority.

Lee sets the tale in Granada, southern Spain in the seventeenth century and focuses on the exploits of a fictional Don Juan figure, Don Juan Gusman del Pulgar, Count of Miramor, who makes a pact with the Virgin Mary in her emanation as 'The Virgin of the Seven Daggers or Lady of Sorrows'.[10] Like his namesake, Lee's Don Juan is a prodigious lover who seeks daringly impossible liaisons, but believes that by dedicating himself to the Virgin of the Seven Daggers he will save himself from going to hell for his sins. Don Juan undertakes one final daring erotic escapade in which he successfully brings back to life a Moorish princess who is buried underneath her enchanted palace, and seeks to win her as his wife. The exquisitely beautiful princess tests his devotion to the Virgin Mary by asking him to declare her more attractive than the Madonna. Don Juan's refusal leads to his execution at the hands of the Infanta's African eunuch. On his death, Don Juan's disembodied spirit wanders the streets of 'Grenada' [sic], comically unaware of his own death. He successfully petitions the Virgin, because of his unfaltering dedication to her, for a place in heaven. The final section of the tale is an epigraph from a fictional letter, written by the real-life Spanish Golden Age dramatist Pedro Calderos de la Barca, in which he commends Don Juan's tale as a pious subject for a dramatic work but one which he, due to old age, will not be able to write himself. The tale concludes with a modern writer claiming authorship of the tale where de la Barca had earlier abandoned it.

Like the tales of the *Hauntings* collection, this is another tale that derives its creative impetus from a troubling sense of cultural disjunction. Figuratively, Don Juan's journey to the princess's underground chamber signals that Spain is founded on, but denies, its historical links with Moorish culture. Above ground, a tense battle between North Africa and southern Spain for dominance of the area is both played out by the elements and manifests itself in the city's architecture. An ornate description of the fictional church of Our Lady of the Seven Daggers in the city suggests that the Virgin's church is less a place of worship than a citadel used to separate European Spain from any African influence. As the narrator describes it, the church roof 'shines barbarically', the church has a 'monstrous front' and as a 'superb example of the pompous, pedantic and contorted architectural style of the later Philips' attests to Spanish imperial hubris. The church is physically unsettling and leaves the mind bewildered by the violent lines of its architectural design in which the viewer can read the history of the brutal repression of the African element by Europe. Lee's description of the church is particularly visceral and she writes of 'jagged lines everywhere as of spikes for exhibiting the heads of traitors; dizzy ledges as of mountain precipices for dashing to bits Morisco rebels; line warring with line and curve with curve; a place in which the mind staggers bruised and half stunned' (*HAOFT*, 249–50). Rather than representing an elegant melding of two cultures, the church reveals the struggle between Africa and Europe for cultural and political dominance of the region and its history as one of violent conflict between two civilizations.

In the tale, the battle for cultural dominance of Southern Spain has its counterpart in the two supernatural women between whom Don Juan must make his choice: the Virgin of the Seven Daggers and the Moorish princess. Lee's description of the statue of the Virgin is eerie and mysterious. To the viewer, her statue appears as a doll with a 'wax' face who wears a voluminous dress made of a 'mysterious russet and violet...silk' in which, menacingly, 'her body is cased like a knife in its sheath' (*HAOFT*, 250). In the preface that she wrote to the 1927 edition of the tale, Lee looks back to the genesis of the story in 1889 and reveals how the Marian subject matter of the story was directly influenced by Baudelaire's poem 'À une Madone' from *Les Fleurs du Mal* (1857), arguably the foundational text of French Decadence. Lee not only uses the subtitle of Baudelaire's poem – 'Ex-voto dans le Goût Espagnol' – as an epigraph for her preface but also tells of how Baudelaire's poem inspired her to write her own 'votive offering in the Spanish style' (*HAOFT*, 243 and 247). In Baudelaire's poem, a tortured lover desires a sacrilegious erotic union with the Virgin Mary and in a torrent of desire he tells the statue of how he wishes to 'Cloth[e] with kisses all your rosy flesh'. 'À une Madone' inverts the 'Seven Daggers' of Marian iconography. Where traditionally the seven knives represent Mary's sorrows, in Baudelaire's poem they represent the seven deadly sins as the lover promises to slake his desire by 'plant[ing]' 'seven bright Daggers' in the Madonna's breast.[11] Yet, in line with the sanitizing tenor of much of her *fin-de-siècle* fiction, we can see that in her story Lee refuses to give herself over to this French Decadent re-imagining of Spain and instead seeks to diminish the tortured and violent desires expressed in Baudelaire's poem. In comparison to Baudelaire's original, what Lee humorously calls her own 'profanity' in bringing Don Juan and the Virgin of the Seven Daggers together in the same story appears intentionally innocuous.

Lee's desire to bowdlerize Baudelaire's provocative poem by specifically censoring its perverse and profane eroticism is mirrored in the intense sense of cultural anxiety that she admits to feeling with regards to Spain. In this tale, we see Lee's special sense of herself as the 'sentimental' and sensitive European traveller unravel when directly confronted both by Spain and Baudelairean Decadence, types of European culture that stood directly outside the elegant and decorous stream of classical and neo-classical culture of Italy and Greece that had shaped her own cultural life. Indeed, Lee's unapologetic assertion in the 1927 preface that this tale was born of her temperamental *aversion* to all things Spanish attests to a less than objective response to Spain on her part. In the preface she writes of her dislike of Spanish art and how she 'detest[s] the melancholy lymphatic Hapsburgs of Velasquez, the lousy, greedy beggars of Murillo, the black and white penitents of Ribera and Zurbaran, [and], above all, the elongated ecstasies and fervent dullards of Greco'. Lee envisions Spanish culture as a fevered mix of '*auto da fés* and bull fights' and presents the nation as one in thrall to cruelty and sensuality. Her description of Spanish Catholicism as a mongrel mix of a moribund and grotesque Oriental influence and a repressive spiritual orthodoxy brings another unnerving layer of hybridity to the text. Here Lee expressly articulates her distaste for Spanish Catholicism and strikingly presents her tale as one founded on a 'detestation for all that Counter-Reformation and especially Spanish cultus of death, damnation, tears and wounds Asiatic *fleurs du Mal* sprung of the blood of Adonis, and taking root in the Spanish mud' (*HAOFT*, 245–6). Disturbingly for Lee, both the examples of Spanish art and religion suggest that Europe carries within its own borders its spiritual and artistic 'other'. And, as a result of this marked refusal on Lee's part to countenance the cultural difference and diversity that Spain represents, the modern reader might begin to question how truly cosmopolitan Lee's identity actually was. In the 1927 preface, Lee also links the tale to the one and only trip that she made to Granada in the winter of 1888. Certainly, the highly-fevered atmosphere of the tale can be explained by Lee's own sense of mental disturbance on this trip, a trip which she admits she had taken to recover from an extended period of 'nervous depression' (*HAOFT*, 246). As noted in the introduction, Lee's nervous illness during this period seems to have resulted from the painful collapse of her relationship with Mary Robinson in 1888. While it is speculative to link this tale of Don Juan's impossible choice between spiritual devotion and human love to Lee's own romantic affairs, such a reading is nonetheless tantalizing. Continuing in this vein, we might even go so far as to link the choice that Don Juan has to make, between the spiritual love of the Virgin and his all too human desire for the princess and her possessions, to Lee's recent involvement in her own love triangle, in which Robinson had chosen the platonic love offered to her by her fiancé James Darmesteter over the passionate love that she had experienced with Lee.

This inventive tale thus feverishly mixes Spain's historical encounter with the Moors to Decadent impiety, pantomime scenes of necromancy, Orientalist fantasies of buried treasure and the mildly profane and comic spectacle of Don Juan's final ascension to heaven. And yet, instead of ending this formally hybrid tale here, the final section of the story closes by focusing on a letter purportedly written by the real-life seventeenth-century Spanish Golden Age dramatist, Pedro Calderos de la Barca, in which he recommends Don Juan's tale to the fictional Archpriest Morales as a subject for a drama to invoke religious piety in unbelievers. Before he can do so, however, an unidentified and 'unworthy modern hand' intervenes to claim that de la Barca died before he could write the narrative and so cleared the way for the 'modern' author to finish it (*HAOFT*, 278).

In mixing fiction, history, authorial anonymity and a Catholic miracle, this incongruous ending both looks back to an inherited English literary tradition of the previous century *and* appears to anticipate experimental writing of the late twentieth century. As first advanced in Horace Walpole's *The Castle of Otranto* (1764), a favoured strategy of the eighteenth-century Gothic novel was to present the supernatural narrative as one written by an anonymous Catholic writer to support the Catholic belief in miracles. This text is then purportedly 'discovered' to have been written by a 'modern' English Protestant writer in a strategy which expressly allowed the English writer to satirize an alien and 'superstitious' Roman Catholic orthodoxy.[12] That Lee likewise explicitly envisioned the tale she wrote as a satire against Roman Catholic orthodoxy supports links between her supernatural tale and what she once called the 'grim and ghastly romances' of the previous century (*E*, 1: 79). Equally, 'The Virgin of the Seven Daggers' can also be seen to look forward to late-twentieth century metafiction such as John Fowles's novel *The French Lieutenant's Woman* (1969) in which the 'author' breaks the illusion of omniscience and thereby, consciously exposes the fictionality of the text. In the closing lines of 'The Virgin of the Seven Daggers', the sense of the original genius and literary authority prized by the writer is explicitly undermined as the 'modern' author tells of how the story is one appropriated from a letter purported to have been written by a celebrated real-life author from a previous century. And again, this narrative strategy appears to anticipate the appearance of the 'author' as a character, as seen in 'John Fowles's' conscious musings on French critic Roland Barthes's celebrated theories of 'the death of the author' which he, in turn, would deploy some forty years later to interrogate the notion of literary authority.[13] Certainly, it seems entirely fitting that Lee's complex, flippantly profane and unsettling super-natural tale should end by casually destabilizing the notion of authority and authenticity.

In the 1927 preface, Lee rounds off her distaste for what she considers to be the alien and unnerving aspects of European culture, that both Baudelairean Decadence and (Moorish) Spain represented, by neutralizing them through her recollection of how the tale was written against the backdrop of the English countryside in the summer of 1889. Here, Lee attempts to assuage the prevalent spirit of Decadent ennui and morbidity which, as we saw in the last chapter, marked the *fin de siècle* with the comfortably familiar English setting of 'a grassy terrace above the Worcestershire Avon' (*HAOFT*, 248). Lee recalls how when writing the tale she was in the company of her childhood friend, the celebrated American painter John Singer Sargent. The fact that both of these artists were, in essence, if not foreigners then certainly not English might suggest that for Lee some modes of cultural mixing and alterity were more acceptable than others.

Finally, it is significant that in the 1927 preface Lee dedicates this incongruous tale to her friend Maurice Baring. That Lee framed her darkly comic vision of European disunity in 'The Virgin of the Seven Daggers' with a dedication which emphasizes the importance of friendship across national, cultural and religious borders, had a resonance with contemporary political events. As we shall see in the readings of Lee's two anti-war plays, *The Ballet of the Nations* (1915) and *Satan the Waster* (1920), that follow in the next chapter, Lee fully articulated her sense that the building of real community would forestall the onslaught of destructive imperial ambitions and the greed of multinational corporations that dominated contemporary European affairs. In the next chapter, we will explore Lee's brave and (largely) isolated response to the First World War and her painful sense of the final destruction of her beloved Europe that it augured. As we shall see, in the twentieth century and, much to Lee's sorrow, her role as a 'sentimental traveller' and as a 'cosmopolitan' intellectual would become both politically suspect and publicly unpopular.[14]

3

'Art Not for Art's Sake'

No full account of Lee's writing or any retrospective assessment of her influence on English letters would be complete without an examination of some of her more controversial and ground-breaking works such as her collaborative research into 'psychological aesthetics' and her two pacifist pieces *The Ballet of the Nations* (1915) and *Satan the Waster* (1920). This chapter opens with an account of the novel, if somewhat eccentric, research that Lee began in the late 1880s with her companion Kit Anstruther-Thomson into the psychological and physiological effects of art. It then explores how the events of the First World War came to politicize Lee's cosmopolitan identity and triggered a change of direction in both her writing and its public reception. And here, we examine the public censure that Lee faced (from H.G. Wells amongst others) for refusing to blame German imperial ambitions alone for the war and how she, in turn, bravely sought to explain her deeply unpopular and avowedly unpatriotic stance in the two anti-war works she wrote. Finally, the study concludes with a reading of Lee's quasi-empirical treatise on the art of good writing *The Handling of Words* (1923) for the revealing insight that it offers into her efforts to adapt to the changing world of twentieth-century letters. In *The Handling of Words*, we see Lee express both her frustration at what she believed to be the degraded literary tastes of post-war audiences and also unexpectedly reveal a sympathetic understanding of the upcoming generation of Modernist writers and their desire to produce experimental, visceral and confrontational works.

PSYCHOLOGICAL AESTHETICS

As we saw in chapter 1, Lee closed the 1895 valedictory to Walter Pater that appeared in *Renaissance Fancies and Studies* by pledging herself memorably to 'art, not for art's sake, but art for the sake of life – art as one of the harmonious functions of existence' (*RFS*, 259). Here, we see Lee not only bid a final farewell to the aestheticism of her youth but, more importantly, publicly announce her desire to discover a socially productive and practical role that art could play in life. Moreover, statements such as 'art is the outcome of a surplus of human energy, the expression of a state of vital harmony' show the 'Valedictory' to be clearly informed by a new and markedly physiological vision of the aesthetic experience in which Lee conceives of art as both a product and an instrument of physical well-being (*RFS*, 253). Significantly, the novel vision of art-appreciation articulated in *Renaissance Fancies and Studies* was not a passing phase in the development of Lee's art–philosophy but instead represented not only a new mode of thinking on her part but also gave the first public indication of the research that she had been undertaking in the field of 'psychological aesthetics' for nearly a decade. And, as we shall see, Lee continued to dedicate both her intellectual *and* emotional energies to refining her research into the psychological and physical effects of art well into the next century.[1]

Lee's theory of 'psychological aesthetics' was inspired by the intensely visceral responses to art experienced by her companion and erstwhile collaborator Kit Anstruther-Thomson in whom Lee found an unusually productive subject for her nascent researches into the psychology of aesthetic response. From 1887 onwards, Lee accompanied Kit through the galleries of Western Europe to watch and listen as her subject painstakingly described the various psychological and physical effects she experienced in front of various *objets d'art* such as Greek statues and pieces of Chippendale furniture, and in buildings such as Gothic cathedrals. Kit proved acutely sensitive to the changes in breathing and the muscular tensions induced by art. She also told Lee how during a viewing she felt that she unconsciously mimicked the posture of a piece, whether a statue or a chair. Moreover, Kit also claimed to experience feelings of physical well-being or discomfort when in the presence of beautiful or ugly things. This suggested to the couple the existence of an intrinsic link between artistic form and good health. By extension, they would later come to use this apparent link to argue that the use of the 'correct' posture when viewing art could induce feelings of mental and physical well-being.

The pioneering work of the German psychologist, Theodor Lipps, on empathy and art was to prove instrumental in the couple's subsequent formalization of their early conjectures into their fully-fledged theory of 'psychological aesthetics'. In his *Raumaesthetik* (1896) Lipps put forward the idea that the aesthetic experience involved the spectator's absolute absorption in the form of the object. According to Lipps (as translated from German by Lee) this experience of empathy (*Einfühlung*) or 'feeling into' the aesthetic form involved a type of inner mimicry in which the viewer mentally projected him or herself into the object. Thus, Lipps wrote 'In aesthetic contemplation I therefore lend to the aesthetic object my own personality in a particular manner, or at all events a mode *of my* personality's existence. The Object, to which I aesthetically lend life or soul, carries in itself a reflection of my personality' (*BU*, 39; emphasis in original). Although, as seen above, Lipps emphatically figured empathy as a process in which the subject projects his or her personality on to the object, Lee erroneously chose to read Kit's description of the visceral impact that art, particularly the plastic arts, had upon her sentient body and her unconscious copying of the pose and posture of the art object as entirely consonant with Lipps's theories of empathy and inner mimicry.

In 1897, after nearly a decade of their gallery research, Kit and Lee showcased their theory of 'psychological aesthetics' in a jointly-authored article entitled 'Beauty and Ugliness' for the prestigious journal the *Contemporary Review*. With reference to works in the field by Grant Allen and Herbert Spencer, Lee conceptualized their findings while it was left to Kit, who appeared under the gender-neutral guise of her initials 'C.A.T.' in the text, to draw on excerpts from the couple's gallery diaries to describe the precise physical sensations produced by various works of art. Thus, 'C.A.T.' explains how looking at a chair affected the movement of her eyes, changed her breathing pattern and made her mime the position of the object with her own stance. Physical sensations were divided into the agreeable and disagreeable with these sensations reflecting beauty and ugliness, respectively. Kit describes how beauty induces tensions of *'lifting up'* and *'pressing downwards'* which, she contends, have the effect of producing an 'agreeable arrangement of agreeable movements in ourselves' constituting 'a harmonious total condition of our adjustments'. Classical statues stood as the epitome of beautiful art and the couple sought to prove that simply the act of looking at Greek sculpture and replicating the stance of the ideal forms on display would enhance the viewer's health. In their extended exposition of the medicinal function of Greek sculpture, Lee contends that the 'antique statue' has a 'much finer muscular system' than a human being and that the act of 'miming' the posture of this perfect form 'gives us the benefit of the finer organism represented'. Looking at the statue elicits a series of 'muscular adjustments' in the 'beholder' where, according to the couple, the 'sight of the easy carriage of body' incarnated by the statue gives the viewer 'a sense of increased lightness and strength' in themselves (*BU*, 184, 221–2; emphasis in original). In their earnest advice to adopt the healthy posture of Greek statues, the couple had misguidedly given Lipps's theory of 'inner mimicry' a literal rendering, a mistake which Lipps himself would point out in an unsympathetic review of their work in 1898 (Colby, 166).

Eminent detractors aside, Kit and Lee, themselves, explicitly envisaged the project to be a serious scientific investigation that would contribute to aesthetics being, in their words, 'recognised as one of the most important and most suggestive parts of the great science of perception and emotion' (*BU*, 157). And, although the research is of an entirely different order to Lee's fiction, conceptually, psychological aesthetics seems to have been conceived by the couple as a new aesthetic theory that expressly offered a practical remedy to the social detachment associated with high art movements, as earlier identified by Lee in *Miss Brown*, *A Phantom Lover* and 'Prince Alberic and the Snake Lady'. Certainly, the way in which the couple described the conceptual remit of the project suggests that through this research Lee and Kit sought to demystify the more hieratic and mystical extremes associated with high art in the public mind.[2] Accordingly, they briskly declare in the introduction that the appreciation of aesthetic form 'implies an *active participation* of the most important organs of *animal life*' and that the desire for beauty is '*no unaccountable psychic complexity*, but the necessary self-established regulation of processes capable of affording disadvantage and advantage to the organism' (*BU*, 157, 225; emphasis added). Here, the reduction of an individual's appreciation of art to no more than an involuntary and instinctive physical response appears to be a further attempt at undermining high art's romantic assertions of the hieratic and mystical power of beauty.

In the readings of *Miss Brown* and *A Phantom Lover* undertaken in chapter 1, we witnessed Lee's exasperation at the way in which the privileged and exclusive art philosophies propounded by Pre-Raphaelite and Aesthetic circles excluded women as active participants and whose commitment to the social question could be described as casual, at best. The couple's commitment to finding a practical remedy for the exclusivity of the 'high art' schools also led them to take their work on psychological aesthetics to the public where Kit demonstrated the method in the public galleries of London to both the couple's upper-class female devotees and to groups of working-class observers.[3] The presence of these different social classes at the gallery demonstrations suggests that the couple pursued a democratic and inclusive art theory which would forestall the further appearance of the kinds of 'aesthetical anarchy' already witnessed at the *fin de siècle* (*RFS*, 255). Later, Lee also took pains to emphasize that Kit's involvement in the project was not that of an aristocratic dilettante but was motivated by long-held 'socialistic' principles. Lee writes:

> Art... could never be in her [Kit's] eyes a mere private pleasure, still less an amusement for leisured folks. She saw it rather as a semi-religious side of life, into which every one, and the disinherited foremost, must be initiated by those who were specially gifted and fortunately circumstanced. [4]

Here, Lee's emotive and almost mystical description of the working classes is telling in its indication that, however well-meaning the two women were, in the end, the class differences between practitioners and participants meant that the philanthropic impact of the project was always to remain limited.

The later addition of another dimension to their research must have made psychological aesthetics appear outlandish to even the most enthusiastic of converts. As Lee was later to recall, Kit discovered that when she hummed certain musical phrases in her head that 'some of them seemed to enhance and others to inhibit (apart from all suggestions of subject or words) the aesthetic perception of visible shapes.' From this, the couple came to believe that like music, visible material forms had the effect of 'altering, unifying, as well as vivifying our moods' and that the effects of perceiving beauty in either material or immaterial forms was an operation that took place in time. As a result, the couple spent the summer of 1894 'sampling' statues by mentally humming tunes in front of them (*AM*, 38).

Perhaps not unsurprisingly, outside observers found the couple's research to be somewhat eccentric and idiosyncratic. In her 1940 autobiography *What Happened Next*, Lee's friend, the suffragette composer Dame Ethel Smyth recalled witnessing the couple's 'sampling' statues method first hand on one of their gallery visits. Smyth's satirical sketch is remorseless:

> To give an illustration of Vernon's method of eliciting pronounce-ments from the oracle, some years ago I had gone with her and Kit to the Vatican, when, pulling up before...[a] bust of Apollo Vernon suddenly said 'Kit! show us that bust!' Kit's proceedings were remarkable; in dead silence she advanced, then retreated, shaded her eyes and finally ejaculated: 'Look at that Johnny! how he sings! ...how he sings!' Various technical details were then pointed out as proving their contention, though Vernon considered these as less important than the 'singing' quality discovered by her friend. And afterwards, when I privately expressed my opinions of this style of Art Criticism, Vernon was very angry and begged me not to 'expose' myself (quoted in Gunn, 157).

The project faced further controversy when in 1898 the American scholar of Renaissance art Bernard Berenson accused the couple of plagiarizing his ideas. Berenson claimed that it was he who had suggested ideas to the couple about the muscular sensations induced on viewing art when accompanying them on their gallery tours. Although the charge was to remain unsubstantiated and was dropped by Berenson within months, it so wounded Kit that she suffered a nervous breakdown as a result. Much to Lee's regret, both the exacting nature of their work and her own growing emotional dependence on Kit, led Kit to abandon the project and separate from Lee in the same year.

Notwithstanding the irreverent and often unsympathetic nature of Smyth's eye-witness description of the couple at work, her account was the first to indicate publicly that the couple's research had an erotic dimension to it. In another volume of her autobiography (*As Time Went On*), Smyth also suggested that Lee habitually used the ploy of collaborative aesthetic research to bind herself to the women to whom she was (unconsciously) attracted (see Colby 176). Recently, and decidedly more sympathetic than Smyth to the complex way in which Lee responded to the women she was attracted to, the critic Kathy Alexis Psomiades has interpreted psychological aesthetics as the product of Lee's sublimated desire for Kit. She argues that in making Kit's bodily sensations pivotal to psychological aesthetics, Lee was substituting 'the beloved's bodily sensations... for a carnal knowledge of that body'.[5] Alternatively, Diana Maltz in her recent account of psychological aesthetics proposes that Kit had a penchant for 'performance' and argues that it was this that led her, rather than Lee, to manipulate her gallery demonstrations into 'a lively, liberated forum for an aristocratic lesbian elite' (Maltz, 213).

While the precise nature of the erotic dynamics of the project can only remain the subject of speculation, scholarly or otherwise, the way in which Lee, herself, chose to memorialize her friend and their collaborative research in *Art and Man* in 1924 is both poignant and candid. Significantly, where in the original *Beauty and Ugliness* articles, Kit's body was figured as gender neutral, in the introduction to *Art and Man* Lee restores the same-sex modality of their work. Lee, who had devoted her life to aesthetics, makes the moving confession that:

> It was only as a result of intimacy with Kit Anstruther-Thomson that I became aware that, much as I had written and even much as I had read about works of art, I did not really know them when they were in front of me... And, becoming aware that, in her sense of *seeing*, I saw half nothing, I tried to learn a little *to see* by looking at her way of looking at things (*AM*, 29–30; emphasis in original).

Strikingly, in the introduction to *Art and Man* we see instinct and empathy explicitly unseat the wholly academic response to art that Lee admits to having previously relied upon. She describes how in attempting to replicate Kit's vision she consciously sought to discount her own academic knowledge in order to allow herself to respond spontaneously to art for the first time. Given the continued anxiety on Lee's part over the reception of women's writing that we have traced in this study, it is significant that in this valedictory to her dead friend Lee aligns herself to, and privileges, a woman's non-academic and intuitive perspective on art. And here, Lee also shows herself to be equally aware that her own academic learning threatened to damage the spontaneous responses to art that Kit had tried to teach by example. 'Kit', Lee writes in *Art and Man*, 'may have felt as if her very personal and living impressions were being deadened under what perhaps struck her as philosophical padding' (*AM*, 53). Lee's sadness and regret that what had been conceived as a curative project should end in physical collapse for her beloved collaborator is palpable.

HOLDING ALOOF: TWO PACIFIST WORKS

While she continued to work alone on her theory of psychological aesthetics into the next century, by 1912 Lee no longer considered the theory to have much scientific validity. In the introduction to *Beauty and Ugliness* she admits that 'my aesthetics will always be those of the gallery and the studio, not of the laboratory. They will never achieve scientific certainty' (quoted in Colby, 155). This *volte-face* on psychological aesthetics was accompanied by Lee's increasing pessimism at the reception of her work more generally. Although she produced what she considered to be some of her best work in the early-twentieth century (she believed her play *Ariadne in Mantua* (1903) and the novel *Penelope Brandling* (1903) to be her finest pieces), changes in public taste made it difficult to place these literary works with publishers. While she remained resolute in following her own intellectual interests throughout her career, rather than the demands of the literary marketplace, by 1906, however, Lee became increasingly aware that the consequence of creative and intellectual freedom was not only a lack of an appreciative audience but also a growing sense of her own intellectual isolation, as she had recognized earlier. She gave the following assessment of her professional career in a letter to Maurice Baring:

> It is certain that I can never imagine what I write being read, still less by anyone in particular. (I know my writings tend more and more towards the soliloquy.) It gives, perhaps, a certain freedom and decency, but sometimes, not often, it makes one feel a bit lonely, as if one were the vox clamans, not in the desert, but inside a cupboard (quoted in Colby, 308–9).[6]

In this candid letter to Baring, Lee links her refusal to compromise her principles and intellectual interests to a neglect or even possible censoring of her public voice. While in 1906, Lee's continued unease about her public reception might have been a little over-dramatic, we shall see how in coming years the anxieties expressed here were actually to prove painfully prophetic.

Lee's interest in exploring the social utility of art that she had begun in the psychological aesthetics project was to take on an urgently political dimension around the events of the Great War of 1914–18. This led her to write, in the face of much public opposition, two formally inventive and politically contentious anti-war works *The Ballet of the Nations* (1915) and *Satan the Waster* (1920). In the previous chapter we saw how at the turn of the twentieth century, Lee's story 'The Virgin of the Seven Daggers' revealed both her distaste for the aspects of European culture that did not conform to classical ideals and her own fear that her role as a 'sentimental traveller' might not confer the special and privileged insight into Europe on which she had founded her professional career. And yet, as we shall see in the reading of Lee's pacifist pieces that follow, as the events of the First World War unfolded she not only made a wholesale reinvestment in her expatriate identity but, importantly, came to ground her pacifism in it. Indeed, the war years saw Lee consistently reiterate that it was precisely her interstitial national identity that allowed her a measure of objectivity. This helped her to remain aloof from the negative and, according to her, irrational demands made upon individuals in the name of patriotism. '[I]s not the respective *national pride* of the Englishman, Frenchman, German, Italian' she had pointedly asked in 1897 'the purest megalomania in guise of patriotism?' (*GA*, 85; emphasis in original).

Lee's passionate and public commitment to peace isolated her from friends such as Mary Robinson, Maurice Baring and Ethel Smyth who were all actively involved in the war effort. At the beginning of the twentieth century, unlike her patriotic British friends, Lee refused to vilify German militarism and imperial ambitions when she believed the allied nations (the United Kingdom, France, Russia and later, Italy) to be guilty of exactly the same expansionist manoeuvres as the Germans. In the build-up to the war, Lee wrote a number of pacifist articles for Ramsay MacDonald's 'Union of Democratic Control' (popularly known as the UDC), a group which sought to temper the aggressively imperialist claims of both the allies and Germany. In 1912, she wrote an article 'The Ethics of Glass Houses' for the *Nation* that reminded Britons, who staunchly disapproved of Germany's aggressive expansionism, of the damage wreaked in living memory by British campaigns in Africa such as those in the Sudan (1896–98) and against the Boers (1880–1 and 1899–1902). In this impassioned article, Lee presents British 'fears' about German expansionism as disproportionate and essentially hypocritical. '[Remember] your various land grabbings – so necessary to the world's progress –' she reminds readers 'and the elimination of sundry backward races; remember the burning of the Boer farms; remember the Concentration Camps; remember the Mahdi's head.' Significantly, as we might have come to expect from Lee, she did not proffer these opinions from the position of an enlightened European intellectual but rather sought to forestall accusations of unpatriotic behaviour on her part by taking up an overtly British national identity and appealing to shared British values of 'sheer spiritual good taste and breeding'. In the following year, Lee wrote another article for the *Nation* ('Lessons of History') in which she warned that Britain 'being a colonising Empire, will duly become the prey of Japanese, Americans, especially of Germans' (quoted in Colby, 287–9). As we can see, not only did Lee remain entirely unconvinced about the 'civilizing' mission of imperialism *per se* but she also presciently saw how the so-called 'Great Game of Empire' had, and would, involve different nations in a series of bloody global conflicts.

Lee was on her annual trip to Britain in August 1914 when war was declared on Germany, an event that meant that she was unable to return home to her beloved Italy for the course of the war. In this year, her pacifist stance and refusal to come out in support of the allies embroiled her in a very public altercation with her friend H. G. Wells in both the New York *Nation* and the *Labour Leader*. Wells was an enthusiastic supporter of the war and had urged the (as yet neutral) United States to boycott trade with Germany, a position which had left Lee quite disgusted that Wells proposed that (in her words) 'America use and show her neutrality by starving Germany' (quoted in Colby, 290). In turn, Wells patronizingly accused Lee of political naïvety and regretted that she had been completely lost to her apparently pro-German sympathies. This heated emotional exchange with Wells led Lee to write a simple and moving allegorical response to both the war and her numerous detractors.

In 'The Heart of a Neutral' Lee imagines her own fairy christening at which all the nations of Europe were present and gave her the gift of loving them all and yet, as with the classic fairy story, one fairy had unwittingly been overlooked in the invitations. In revenge, this neglected fairy cursed the baby with 'the knowledge of the good of each nation' but also 'the weakness and folly of them all'. Lee describes how a good fairy then intervened and balanced out this curse with her own gift. 'When all the nations shall welter in the pollution of warfare,' as Lee describes the fairy's gift 'this child's eyes shall remain clear from its fratricide fumes; she shall drink deep of sorrow, but recognise and put away from her lips the sweetened and consecrated cup of hatred'.[7] As her beloved Europe imploded under what she perceived to be fratricidal urges, we see Lee imbue her cosmopolitanism with a moral authority of near mythic dimensions. Self-evidently, anti-German feeling, patriotism and support for the war was not limited to Lee's British readers alone and her continued and vocal distaste for the behaviour of the allies led to her public denouncement by the French writer Augustine Bulteau that year. Ironically, it was Lee's pacifist cosmopolitanism and her commitment to European unity that had now jeopardized her professional standing in Europe.

In 1915, Lee went on to write another short prose-piece, *The Ballet of the Nations*, to protest again against the war which was now underway. Illustrated by the artist Maxwell Arnfield with lithographs of veiled classical figures, Lee's *Ballet* envisages the war as a performance staged by Satan with the aid of his Ballet Master, Death, in 'The Theatre of the West' for the purposes of his own amusement. Death gathers together an Orchestra of Human Passions which is variously made up of Widow Fear, her 'shabby, restless twins Suspicion and Panic', Lady Idealism and Prince Adventure, Death's mother Sin, 'her well-known crew' Rapine, Lust, Murder, Famine and the siblings Hatred and Self-Righteousness who are 'fitted out with bull-roarers and rattles and other cannibalistic instruments'. The Passions are joined on stage by twentieth-century newcomers Madam Science and Councillor Organisation who are similarly furnished with a gramophone and miniature pianola with which they, too, are instructed to rouse the Nations with 'archaic' and yet simultaneously 'ultra-modern music' which is pointedly offset by 'allied harmonies and powerful national unisons'. The nations enter in pairs and, before a gathered audience of 'the Ages to Come', dance the first figure of the ballet, 'the Defence of the Weak', in which, the smallest nation is pounded to a pulp. The remaining nations then turn to attack each other in an orgy of violence which leaves the stage littered with 'spirts of blood and pellets of human flesh'. The maimed nations continue to dance to the point where only the Head, a figurative representation of the collective governments of the warring nations, survives intact. Behind the dancers the scene slowly changes from 'the tender radiance of an August sunset above half-harvested fields' to a landscape scarred with 'exploding munition-magazine, while overhead flutter and whir great wings which shower down bomb-lightnings.' Satan gloats that he 'prefers' this piece to 'the other mystery-plays, like Earthquake and Pestilence, which Death puts on our stage from time to time' because 'it gives [the players] immense scope for moral beauty, and revives religious feeling in all its genuine primeval polytheism'. When the Orchestra of Human Passions begins to flag, Satan brings on Pity and Indignation to inspire the nations to a fresh round of killing. *The Ballet* ends inconclusively with Lee's urbane Satan planning its perpetual run (*BN*, 11–12, 16, 21–25).

In 1915, as the events of the war unfolded around her, Lee urgently sought with her *Ballet* to contest ennobling justifications for the war by presenting it as inherently barbaric, destructive and, more importantly for her, wholly avoidable. As Lee controversially presents it, patriotic sentiment and the capacity for self-sacrifice and heroism which war both engenders and exploits are emphatically ignoble and, to her, are indicative of mass 'spiritual inertia' and, even more damningly, 'the need for self-respect' (*SW*, xlv). Stylistically, by imagining the war as a grotesquely violent dance accompanied by atonal music, *The Ballet of the Nations* edges towards the experimental and the avant–garde. Politically radical and artistically inventive, this short work articulates Lee's dissident pacifism in an electrifyingly discordant and dissonant modern idiom.

Although the powerful central conceit of *The Ballet* needed little explanation, Lee retrospectively returned to the work post-Armistice and, in 1920, she extended *The Ballet* by attaching a prologue, epilogue, full commentary and introduction to it and published the work as *Satan the Waster*. In this new version, Lee both emphasizes the performative nature of the war by actually rewriting the prose narrative of *The Ballet* as an actual play and introduces it with her public justification for her deeply controversial and unpopular pacifist stance. As she makes clear in the introduction to *Satan the Waster*, Lee believed that both her expatriate national identity and her now highly visible public role as a pacifist had afforded her a privileged, if painfully isolated, insight into the war. 'Being what I am' she recalled of the war years 'I had to hold aloof and holding thus aloof I have been able to see the war under a certain angle and in certain of its aspects which would have been hidden from me had I, as the phrase goes, *been in it*'. Unlike the majority of her compatriots, and to Lee's regret the majority of her friends, this 'holding aloof' made her see the war underway as 'gigantically cruel, but at the same time needless and senseless like some ghastly "Grand Guignol" performance' (*SW*, xviii, vii; emphasis in original).

In the introduction to this new work, Lee gave a retrospective explanation of her motivation for writing the *Ballet* and her individual perspective on the build-up and post-Armistice fallout from the war. In addition, she imparted her thoughts on the psychology of warfare and the hostility that she had, and continued to suffer, by having dared to challenge the war in the first place. The introduction becomes the site of a battle between what Lee sees as her own clear-sighted pacifism and what she considers to be the universal manipulation of public opinion in the name of patriotism, an attitude she regrets had compromised the integrity of those closest to her. In Lee's resolute refusal to apologize for the 'offence which the contents of this volume have already given and are likely to give for yet a while', it would seem that the sense of public disapproval directed at her apparently 'hostile aloofness' had only worked to strengthen her resolve in her pacifist beliefs. In the introduction to the play, Lee tells of how the deepest sense of regret that she felt had been caused by the fact that 'unfortunately' many of her friends could be numbered amongst her detractors (SW, xii–xiii). More especially, she shows how deeply affected she is by the hypocrisy and self-deception of friends who had been uncomfortable with the war but still participated in it and now questioned her right to speak about it. And yet, notwithstanding her own deep sense of personal anguish, Lee responds creatively to the sense of isolation and betrayal that the war induced by suggesting that globally, political and racial difference could be seen as the basis of a new post-colonialist world order for the twentieth century.

As with her articles for the *Nation*, Lee was unapologetic in situating her artistic authority and political integrity in her cosmopolitan world view and the avowedly unpatriotic behaviour that her expatriate identity had engendered. While the events of the First World War had given a new moral and political force to her interstitial national identity they had also clearly shown her how isolating being a citizen of 'Cosmopolis' could actually be under present conditions.[8] In the introduction to *Satan the Waster* she tells her reader, that the war had both 'made me know, admire, love, but also mistrust, several nationalities' and had also made her 'incapable of identifying myself with the whole of any [country]'. This personal sense of alienation from which she was suffering appears to her to have been just a microcosm of the separatist urges that she identified as underpinning all patriotic sentiment and which, she argues, had ultimately led to the war. Lee optimistically envisages the way in which cultural and racial difference could be transformed into the foundation of a new kind of global altruism where, in future years, nations would embrace rather than exploit cultural diversity. (As we shall see, one scene in the epilogue pointedly shows a European academic doctoring his research in order to be able to open up new markets in Africa.) For Lee, the ethical alternative to the imperialist manoeuvres of First World nations suggested itself through the universal 'recognition of the other (for *alter* is Latin for *other*), sides, aspects, possibilities and requirements of things and people'. Lee closes the introduction with an appeal from her 'superannuated self' to younger generations to consider the waste of material and human resources that war brings about and how future generations might work to prevent it (*SW*, xvii, 79, xlvii, l).

Unlike the short prose narrative of the 1915 *Ballet, Satan the Waster* is scripted as a play. In the prologue the audience is taken to Hell and given an insight into the Waster's psychological motivations for manipulating the Human Passions to perform acts of blood-thirsty warmongering. (He tells Clio, the Muse of History, that war starts because he has never felt love (*SW*, 10).) This new prologue prefaces the horrific spectacle to come with a disconcertingly jaunty introductory scene which jars with the grotesque horror of the ballet that follows. In her inventive characterization of Satan as an urbane impresario who directs a band of hopelessly uncoordinated and obtuse performers, we see Lee engage in a form of self-reflexive theatricality ('meta-theatre') and deploy the dramatic technique performance within a performance. Here, Lee's experimental technique both looks back to Shakespeare's mechanicals from *A Midsummer Night's Dream* and anticipates the highly developed self-conscious humour of late twentieth-century comedy such as that now most closely associated with the early work of the British playwright Tom Stoppard in plays such as *Rosencrantz and Guildenstern are Dead*.

In the new version of the ballet, the Passions (Greed, Loyalty, Discipline, Comradeship, Jealousy, Egotism, Bullying, Ennui and others) and twentieth-century newcomers Madam Science and Councillor Organisation, now form an 'Orchestra of Patriotism'. Again, the music the Orchestra performs is consciously dissonant and has 'conflicting rhythms' because (as Death directs) 'such incoherence conduces to the volume and impressiveness of the patriotic whole'. At Satan's side sits Clio who narrates the performance to a gathered audience of the

'Ages-to-Come' who, pointedly, are not allowed to witness the ballet first-hand. Lee directed that the play was meant to be read out aloud and that no action was to take place on stage. In her notes to the work, Lee wrote that if *Satan the Waster* was ever to be actually staged then it was her 'imperative wish' that 'no attempt be made at showing the Dancing of the Nations' and that 'none of the music must be audible except the voice and drum of Heroism' because actually seeing and hearing it would, according to her, be 'hideous' (*SW*, 42, 57). In 1920, it would seem that the pressure on artistic expression that the war exerted had left Lee no choice but to choose inarticulacy as the most powerful expression of her political beliefs. That the audience is not allowed to see nor hear the ballet the Nations perform appears to function as a conscious figure of Lee's struggle with representing these cataclysmic events. In a strategy that now seems wholly postmodern in its conception, the effect of the (new) ballet is directed at forestalling the representation of the very thing (war) that it contests. Through its absence, this imagined performance conveys emphatically Lee's paradoxical sense of the unrepresentable and yet wholly choreographed and engineered horrors of the war. Moreover, the physical distance that Lee puts in place between her actual audience, the audience of 'the Ages to Come' and the violent dance of the nations suggests that she simultaneously wishes her audience to step back from the performance and to respond to it as objectively as possible. Lee's explicit refusal to represent *per se* is an attempt to divest this brutal spectacle of any sense of tragic gravitas and thus prevent the audience from indulging in the aesthetic and emotional response to the war.

Throughout *Satan the Waster*, Lee inverts notions of both tragedy and burlesque and audience and players in an innovative manner. While her actual audience are asked to see the war as a ridiculous performance, the dancers perform the ballet with entire seriousness because, as Satan explains to Clio 'this ludicrous side always escapes those who take part in [the ballet], for if they saw the full absurdity, they would refuse to act these frightful scenes' (*SW*, 23). And yet as much as the audience is given this privileged insight into the war, by seeing it as a ridiculous burlesque, that the dancing nations do not have, in reality, their own recent participation in this very war elides the (moral) distance between audience and performers. In this way, *Satan the Waster* simultaneously invites and refutes identification between the audience and the dancers, a strategy which allows the audience to reflect, with the benefit of hindsight, on their own role in, and compliance with, the war.

The epilogue of *Satan the Waster* is a breathtaking tour-de-force that features various media and a cast of nations to reveal what the Waster identifies as 'the hidden enigmas underlying the ... Ballet of the Nations'. In the epilogue, Lee reaffirms her commitment to avant-garde performance by incorporating the new media of gramophone and film recordings into the last scenes. Here, a 'half-dozen Supermen of business and commerce' (satirically, Satan judges them to be 'horribly *bourgeois*') are shown to be the real perpetrators of the war. The film and gramophone discs record hypocrisy, collusion and self-deception at all levels of society. The discs play back scenes such as a Frenchman backing the Russians to 'liberate' Alsace from the Germans, the underhand workings of the International Armament Trust (here, a German director proclaims that 'we want a good European war to break up these precious pacifists, and put the rest of them in prison') and an English vicar persuading his mother to invest in arms as the arch-deacon has. The 'Usual Minister' pushes for war because 'this will embroil us with our neighbours. ... It means new alliances, increased armaments. It may end in a European war'. The irrational and naïve patriotism that Lee believed that governments exploit for the purposes of warmongering is dramatized in a disc that shows crowds heedlessly crying out that they will fight to the 'last drop of blood' for 'lasting peace'. A possible end to all conflict is signalled when Heroism wakes up and throws the Ballet Master to the footlights. Satan consoles Death with the idea that future performances can be salvaged by re-clothing him in a 'democratic wig, a complete suit of newest idealistic cut, [which] may make him still pass muster for a while'. This play ends on a slightly more optimistic note than its predecessor as Satan expresses his anxiety that the blind boy Heroism might still find out what a 'preposterous, indecent, anachronism' the Ballet Master is and stop all future ballets. Retrospectively, Lee clearly hoped that a clear assessment of past events would bring humanity to penetrate the 'Vitalizing Lies' of governments and multinational corporations (*SW*, 64, 66, 72–3, 80, 105–6, 109–110, 8; emphasis in original).

Both Hilary Fraser and Vineta Colby have suggested that Lee's anti-war works anticipate the avant-garde modernist strategies of Dada and expressionist theatre (Colby, 305). Although Fraser admits that we can not be sure whether Lee knew about the first Dada performances in Zurich in 1916, equally she feels that similarities between Dadaist performance and Lee's plays are too suggestive to overlook. For Fraser:

> [the] purpose [of Dada] was, through the medium of art – music, dance manifestos, poetry, pictures, posters, costume – to cut across the barriers erected by nationalism and war, and speak to other independent spirits.... [R]adical Dadaist performance, with their beating drums, chanting voices, and allegorical dances, their masks and their verses without words, seems so anarchically in tune with... [Lee's] own *Ballet'*.[9]

And yet, while her commitment to upholding the importance of a cosmopolitan outlook in art and politics appears to place Lee in the company of one of the most radical artistic movements of the early twentieth century, her own abiding memory of this pacifist work is that of a final collaboration that it engendered. In *Art and Man*, Lee recalls:

> And it will always be a dear and significant remembrance to me that, after we had long ceased to work together about other things, Kit's and my last act of collaboration, perhaps the *consummation of our original perfect understanding in all the fundamental matters of life*, was when somewhere in 1915 or 1916 Kit took the chair at a humble UDC meeting in Chelsea, where I read the symbolical fantasia which afterwards grew into my *Satan the Waster* (*AM*, 62; emphasis added).

To Lee, the questions about the social utility of art first addressed in those gallery experiments of the 1880s and 90s were finally consummated some thirty years later in *Satan the Waster*, a work which saw her bring art out of the privileged arena of the gallery and assert its vital ethical and political imperative to younger generations.

VALEDICTORY: *THE HANDLING OF WORDS*

In 1923, Lee published *The Handling of Words* in which she brought together (in her own words) 'disconnected essays and lectures' she had written over the past thirty years and also '[h]alf a lifetime of additional reading and writing, and of ruminating over what I have read and have written'. And yet, the work is not a memoir about youthful and influential associations with late-Victorian literary personalities, such as those written later by her contemporaries W. B. Yeats and Richard Le Gallienne, but rather is a study of the art of good prose-writing. Belying her self-appointed 'superannuated' status, *The Handling of Words* proves to be another pioneering work from Lee in which this time she promised to examine the 'all-important and universally neglected' question which she believed fundamentally defined the art of writing: the relationship between reader and writer. In this ground-breaking text and for the first time in the history of English letters, Lee offered a unique focus on the reading experience and counselled that her audience 'learn what good writing is in order to become the best possible Readers' (*HW*, vii–viii, 33).

Critics Vineta Colby and Christa Zorn have considered the ways in which *The Handling of Words* anticipates modern 'reader-response theory', the critical theory concerned with the different ways in which a reader participates in the reading experience, most recently associated with the work of the American critic, Stanley Fish. Colby credits Lee with discussing 'the dynamics of reading' before the term became current in modern critical theory and has written of the way that the text anticipates the critical writings of I. A. Richards, the Russian formalists, Mikhail Bakhtin, Wolfgang Iser and Roland Barthes (Colby, 200).[10] Christa Zorn has recuperated the text's unique historical position in British criticism finding, as she does, that it 'offers us a glimpse back into the disciplinary transformation of literary criticism, just before it became the province of modernist and postmodernist theories'.[11] Alternatively, the reading that follows situates *The Handling of Words* at another historical crossroads where, as we shall see, Lee uses excerpts from prose writers of the previous century such as George Eliot, Robert Louis Stevenson, Thomas Carlyle and Henry James as examples of good writing in order to reorient what she considered to be the degraded reading tastes of post-war audiences. Lee understood that modern audiences were faced with a choice between either a visceral and disturbing 'Dionysian' art or its binary opposite, the 'lucid truthful vision' and 'healing joy' of 'Apollonian' [sic] art and critically, she believed that the future of contemporary literature was entirely dependent upon the choices that modern readers made (*HW*, 315). By offering the reading public a technical guide to good writing in this final major work, in *The Handling of Words*, Lee appeared to have engineered a final *rapprochement* between herself and what, as we have seen, she had long considered to be an untutored and unappreciative British audience.

Throughout *The Handling of Words*, we are struck by Lee's sense that the best writers induced vigorous and proactive mental exertions from the reader. For example, in her chapter 'On Literary Construction' Lee writes of her admiration for the way in which the novels of Stendhal, Thackeray and Tolstoy make the reader work to understand the narrative rather than allowing a passive relationship to develop between themselves and the text. The 'activity of the Reader' Lee notes 'when he makes a sufficiently complete response, is stimulated and kept alive by the swiftness and certainty demanded of it, and by the constant need for perceiving and co-ordinating a variety of items' (*HW*, 232). Significantly for Lee, the most exemplary formal method used by writers is the one that best facilitates an efficient and logical articulation of ideas. Lee writes:

> Construction, that is to say, co-ordination...means finding out what is important and unimportant, what you can afford and cannot afford to do. It means thinking out the results of every movement you set up in the Reader's mind, how that movement will work into, help, or mar the other movements which you have set up there already, or which you will require to set up there in the future (*HW*, 6).

As we can see from the above passage, Lee considers the well-written text to be one that achieves structural equanimity both in itself and in the reader's mind. In many ways, Lee's emphasis in this passage on 'co-ordination' as a key factor in the reading process recalls the healthful and enlivening physiological vision of art that she had advocated in her theory of psychological aesthetics some thirty years earlier. Vineta Colby has cited the following passage from *The Handling of Words* as evidence that Lee directly redeployed her earlier work on aesthetic empathy for this new work on the reading experience:

> A page of literature whatever its subject-matter, gives us the impression of movement in proportion as it makes us move, not forwards merely, but in every direction; and in such manner as move not forwards merely, but in every direction; and in such manner as to return back on the parts and fold them into unity (*HW*, 232; quoted in Colby, 201).

As Colby identifies above, there are evident connections between the psychological aesthetics project and the conceptual remit of *The Handling of Words*. However, it is worth noting that Lee points out that empathy in the reading experience could only have a psychological rather than the literal physical rendering earlier suggested in the psychological aesthetics project. She writes of how 'literature, whenever it is a free art and not merely a useful process, is the art of evoking in the Reader images and feelings similar to those which outer circumstances have evoked, and inner peculiarities have brought forward, in the Writer'(*HW*, 35). In this passage, Lee now reads empathy as a reciprocal process that involves both the psychological responses of the reader and the writer.

In later chapters entitled 'Studies in Literary Psychology' and 'The Handling of Words', Lee takes a group of randomly selected passages from firstly, three early nineteenth-century prose writers (Thomas De Quincey, Walter Savage Landor, Thomas Carlyle) and secondly, six late-Victorian novelists (George Meredith, Rudyard Kipling, Robert Louis Stevenson, Thomas Hardy, Henry James and Maurice Hewlett) to trace the writer's stylistic habits and the linguistic patterns deployed to 'manipulate' the reader's mind. In her reading of *The Handling of Words*, Christa Zorn astutely observes that 'Behind the quasi-objective study, there is a search for an encounter with human feeling and thought, tied up in continual and individual practices of style' and, as we see below, Lee's comments on individual writers offset her statistical analysis with a profoundly affective vision of the ways in which writers communicate their emotions to readers (Maxwell and Pulham, 188).

Intriguingly, in her examination of Romantic prose writing by De Quincey, Savage Landor and Carlyle, Lee does not explore the writers' use of literary figures and tropes but rather considers how the form of a sentence can be crafted to convey emotion. In this vein, some of Lee's analysis is particularly suggestive. For example, she speculates in a section entitled 'The Syntax of De Quincey' that 'there may be some necessary connection between the structure of a man's sentences and his more human characteristics' (*HW*, 136). Here, we see Lee ask the reader to approach the sentence in a manner akin to poetic form and we might interpret such a move as signalling the desire, on her part, to raise prose to the relatively high artistic status accorded to poetry. It seems germane to point out that while Lee never wrote poetry herself, both her brother and friends such as Mary Robinson and Amy Levy had notable reputations as poets.

This apparent desire to elevate the status of prose is consolidated in the next section of 'Studies in Literary Psychology' entitled 'The Rhetoric of [Walter Savage] Landor' where Lee appears to apply Pater's famous dictum from *The Renaissance* that '*All art constantly aspires toward the condition of music*' to Landor's sentence structure which she approvingly tells her reader she finds 'both musically and grammatically often a wonder'. On 'Carlyle and the Present Tense' Lee concludes that Carlyle used the present tense because it is 'universal' and 'immediate' and, because his writing is characteristically Romantic in tenor, it is 'the tense of the eternal verities, which, from their very nature, have not *been*, but, like all divine things, always *are*' (Pater, 86; *HW*, 164, 186; emphasis in original). Examining three novelists in ensuing sections, Lee's method is both quantitative and qualitative as she not only classifies and counts up the parts of speech from nouns and pronouns to adjectives and adjectival participles used, but also deploys this method to assess the author's control of his syntax. While, in a passage from *Tess of the D'Urbervilles*, Thomas Hardy appears slapdash and illogical to Lee, she judges Henry James's control of his material in *The Ambassadors* as masterful (*HW*, 230, 248).

In the chapter 'The Nature of the Writer' Lee abandons the exploration of the psychological effects of literature through statistical analysis seen in earlier chapters to launch instead a polemic against the state of modern literature. She opens this chapter by asserting the socially productive role that literature should play in society since, according to her, 'only the art of words can thus enlarge our moral and intellectual life, and only it, therefore', she observes 'has a right to the price of such expansion of experience and understanding' (*HW*, 98). And yet, as Lee sees it, the reading tastes of contemporary audiences simply did not support or develop the ethical and experiential power that she specifically associates with literature over the other arts. This new focus on the reader's formative impact on the production of literature rather than *vice versa* leads an exasperated Lee to declare:

> The plain truth is that the bulk of mankind as at present existing, educated mankind quite as much as uneducated, has no use for the finer kind of literature. ...Now, in our very imperfect civilization, most people, even among the well-endowed and energetic, are too fagged, and even among the idle are too busy for any such process (*HW*, 94).

According to Lee, disappointingly, the onward march of modernity and progress had led not only to an enervated and imperfect civilization but also to the production of inferior and sluggish literary works.

Lee continues the essay's striking qualitative judgement of *the reading public* by dividing it into those who approach literature with reverence 'for whom literature really exists [and] who go to it very much as to science or religion' and those who lazily expect easy gratification from the books that they read: 'the Poor in Spirit' or 'The child, the savage or the diseased person'. To Lee, 'The lewdest and most brutal literature is always the least excellent'; and, damningly, she suggests that the less discerning a reader is, the more he will 'naturally magnify all traces' of this 'lower' element. She also attempts to understand whether 'lewd' and 'brutal' literature might have a place in society by applying the two central critical terms utilized by the German philosopher Friedrich Nietzsche in *The Birth of Tragedy* (1873) to explore the effects that art had on audiences. Famously, in this text, Nietzsche had distinguished between the visceral and stirring impact of music as Dionysian and the cool rationality of Apollonian art forms like Greek sculpture. In her conclusion

Lee optimistically invests in Apollonian art as 'an instrument of lucid truthful vision, of healing joy, and perchance even of such prophecy as makes itself come true'. Significantly she does nonetheless allow that the 'fumes and agonies' of Dionysian art might have some socially productive role to play in the continued development of society (*HW*, 101, 94, 315, 113). From a brief survey of her personal library (now housed by the British Council at Florence), we can ascertain that Lee had read the novels of James Joyce and D. H. Lawrence and we might further speculate that her references to the 'excessive or painful emotion' induced by modern examples of Dionysian art could be a reference to the kind of sexually permissive, visceral and experimental literature with which these writers were associated. Despite the antipathy she acknowledges towards such art, she also takes pains to stress that such literature has a value which could only be truly appreciated by a minority of select readers: 'a small number who are the very opposite of that multitude I have dealt with as the Poor in Spirit'. Her characterization of Dionysian artists as 'voluntary and destined martyrs' whose capacity for suffering and tragic self-knowledge invoke awe in their fellow man, also sees her admit that there might be 'room for certain exceptions, dangerous but salutary' in the canons of literature (*HW*, 113). While Lee's brief consideration of Dionysian art finishes on an undecided note, it would seem that for her, somewhat begrudgingly, a provocative art was necessary for exceptional artists and especially responsive readers, to undertake the development of mankind as it had been at the Victorian *fin de siècle*. Her own anxiety about the philistine backlash to Wilde had seen her write in her highly-encoded Decadent fairytale 'Prince Alberic and the Snake Lady' in his defence.[12] On a private level, this cautiously sympathetic understanding of the necessity of a powerfully revolutionary art also seems to have masked a private affinity that Lee felt with Modernist artists. In 1932 she came to regret privately that old age and infirmity now prevented (in her own words) 'all possibility of personal contact with the generation *to which I ought to have belonged*' (quoted in introduction to *HAOFT*, 27; emphasis added).

In her fine reading of *The Handling of Words* Christa Zorn shows how the text articulates 'a deeply romantic longing for retrieving an almost mythical process that connects writer and reader, and human history over time' (Maxwell and Pulham, 188). And here it is significant that in her exposition of her craft that the most important figure that Lee chooses to memorialize in words and seeks to connect with is not a Renaissance artist or one of the great writers of the previous century but her own mother. The penultimate essay of *The Handling of Words* contains a candid description of Mrs Paget who had died thirty years earlier. She was, according to Lee, 'tyrannical and self-immolating...overflowing with sympathy and ruthlessly unforgiving; dreadfully easily wounded and quite callous of wounding others; she was deliciously tender, exquisitely humorous, extraordinarily grim and, at moments, terrifying; always difficult to live with and absolutely adorable'. Lee recalls how Mrs Paget's ambitions for her daughter were grand ('I had to become, at the very least, another De Staël'), and she now admits that looking 'into my literary preferences I find that I care for a good deal of what I have read, and even for some of what I myself have written, because in some indirect manner, it is associated with her indescribable, incomparable person' (*HW*, 300–1). In the final instance, in her summing up of a life in letters, it is significant that Lee looks back to her mother and dedicates her whole career to her. For a woman whose career was profoundly shaped by her anxieties about the reception of women's writing, it seems peculiarly fitting that, in summing up her own achievements, Lee publicly asserts that the most significant influence on her was her mother and the intellectual inheritance that she had bequeathed her.

Notes

INTRODUCTION

1. See Irene Cooper Willis's introduction to *Vernon Lee's Letters*, p. iii, Gunn, 74–5, Colby, 41–2 and Christa Zorn, *Vernon Lee: Aesthetics, History & the Victorian Female Intellectual* (Athens, Ohio: Ohio University Press, 2003), xvii. References to Zorn hereafter in the text.
2. Martha Vicinus, *Intimate Friends: Women Who Loved Women* (2004) (Chicago and London: University of Chicago Press, 2006), 154–6, 234, 162. References to Vicinus hereafter in the text.
3. See Phyllis Grosskurth, *John Addington Symonds: A Biography* (London: Longmans, 1964), 223n.
4. Catherine Maxwell and Patricia Pulham, 'Introduction' to *Vernon Lee: Decadence, Ethics, Aesthetics* (Houndmills, Basingstoke: Palgrave Macmillan, 2006), 3. References to Maxwell and Pulham hereafter in the text.
5. Hilary Fraser, 'Interstitial Identities: Vernon Lee and the Spaces In-Between', in Marysa Demoor (ed.) *Marketing the Author: Authorial Personae, Narrative Selves and Self-Fashioning, 1880–1930* (Houndmills, Basingstoke: Palgrave Macmillan, 2004), 114–15; Fraser's emphasis.
6. Lee fondly recalls her experiences of being educated by German governesses in her essay 'In Praise of Governesses', describing them as 'our spiritual foster mothers who put a few drops of the milk of German kindness, of German simplicity and quaintness and romance, between our lips when we were children', Lee, *Hortus Vitae, Essays on the Gardening of Life* (London and New York: John Lane, The Bodley Head, 1903),15; quoted in Colby, 8.
7. Laurel Brake, 'Vernon Lee and the Pater Circle' in Maxwell and Pulham, 40.
8. Lee wrote that Ruskin 'perceives that pleasure in art is more or less sensuous and selfish; he is afraid lest some day he be called upon to account for the moments he has not given to others, and be chastised for having permitted his mind to follow the guidance of his senses', *B*, 225.

CHAPTER 1. VERNON LEE AND 'HIGH ART'

1. Encounters include the painter James McNeill Whistler suing Ruskin for libel for his negative comments about his painting *Nocturne in Black and Gold: The Falling Rocket* in 1877, and the prosecution of the publisher Henry Vizetelly in 1889 for obscene libel for translating Émile Zola's naturalist novel *La Terre* into English. After reissuing Zola's collected works the following year, Vizetelly was imprisoned for three months and in 1892 the government censor refused to give Wilde's play *Salomé* a public licence. On the public's self-proclaimed philistinism see, for example, the poems 'Concerning a Misused Term; viz, "Art" as Recently Applied to a Certain Form of Literature' and 'A Philistine Paean; Or, the Triumph of the Timid One' that both appeared in *Punch* during the Wilde trials (13 Apr 1895; 11 May 1895); quoted in Kirsten MacLeod, *Fictions of British Decadence* (Houndmills, Basingstoke: Palgrave Macmillan, 2006), 139–40. References to MacLeod hereafter in the text.

2. The PRB had come together in order to challenge the dominance of neo-classical convention in art. Unlike their contemporaries, this group of artists modelled their work on the principles of medieval art and design. The group first attracted controversy in 1850 at the exhibition of Millais' painting *Christ in the House of His Parents* when reviewers, most notably Charles Dickens, were offended by the painting's apparently seedy and ugly naturalism in its representation of Christ and his family.

3. Robert Buchanan, 'The Fleshly School of Poetry', *Contemporary Review*, 18 (Aug–Nov 1871), 343, 338. References to Buchanan hereafter in the text.

4. Quoted in Leonée Ormond, 'Vernon Lee as a Critic of Aestheticism in *Miss Brown*', *Colby Library Quarterly* 9 (Sept. 1970), 136.

5. In response to the publisher Longman's suggestion that she should write a novel, Lee commented in 1881, 'Think if I were a novelist! But even had I time, I should shrink from writing what would certainly be vastly inferior to my other work', quoted in Gunn, 98.

6. Gail Marshall, *Actresses on the Victorian Stage. Feminine Performance and the Galatea Myth* (Cambridge University Press, 1998), 29; references to Marshall hereafter in the text.

7. The Pygmalion myth was first told by the Roman poet Ovid in his *Metamorphosis* who wrote of how the artist Pygmalion was so disgusted by the female sex that he decided to sculpt his ideal of the perfect woman. He fell in love with the statue and begged the Goddess Venus to bring it to life which she did.

8. Marshall analyses poems such as Arthur Hallam's 'Lines Spoken in the Character of Pygmalion' (1832), novels like Thomas Hardy's *The Well-Beloved* and paintings such as Burne-Jones's *Pygmalion and the Image* for their use of the myth. In her reading of *Miss Brown*, Marshall glosses Hamlin's self-mythologization as Pygmalion to Anne's Galatea as a moment in which 'the personality of Anne Brown is obliterated. The desired woman is intensely vulnerable to the sculptor-like attentions of her lover', Marshall, 18–21, 13.

9. Buchanan wrote: 'It is on the score that these tricks and affectations have procured the professors a number of imitators, that the fleshly school deliver their formula that great poets are always to be known because their manner is immediately reproduced by small poets, and that a poet who finds few imitators is probably of inferior rank – by which they mean to infer that they themselves are very great poets indeed', Buchanan, 346.

10. Oscar Wilde, *The Picture of Dorian Gray* (1890, 1891), *Collins Complete Works of Oscar Wilde*, (Glasgow: HarperCollins, 1999), 17. References to Wilde hereafter in the text.

11. See, for example, the argument between Beth Haldane and the aesthete Alfred Cayley Pounce in Sarah Grand's *The Beth Book: Being a Study from the Life of Elizabeth Caldwell Maclure, a Woman of Genius* (London: William Heinemann, 1898), 467 and also Olive Schreiner's staging of an encounter between a New Woman and a politician who is in love with her in 'The Buddhist Priest's Wife' (written in 1891) repr. in *Daughters of Decadence, Women Writers of the Fin-de-Siècle* (ed.) Elaine Showalter (London: Virago, 1993), 84–97.

12. Martha Vicinus, 'The Adolescent Boy: Fin-de-Siècle Femme Fatale?', *Journal of the History of Sexuality*, 5 (1994–5), 92.

13. A bemused Ethel Smyth recalled how Lee hectored Smyth's vicar with protestations that 'woman's love is so essentially *maternal*, that it were tedious to enumerate possible deviations from this basic character; whereas man's love, as obviously and invariably, is *triune*; that is, acquisitive, possessive and BESTIAL!' quoted in Gunn, 134; emphasis in original.

14. For ease of access, all textual references to *A Phantom Lover: A Fantastic Story* (Edinburgh and London: William Blackwood and Sons, 1886) in this chapter refer to the reprinted version of the story which appears as 'Oke of Okehurst: Or, The Phantom Lover' in *Hauntings and Other Fantastic Tales*, (eds.) Catherine Maxwell and Patricia Pulham (Peterborough, Canada: Broadview Press, 2006), 105–153; 'Our Library Table', *Athenaeum*, 3070 (Aug 26, 1886), 271; William Wallace, *The Academy*, 747 (Aug 28, 1886), 134.

15. Vernon Lee to Matilda Paget, July 15 1886, Vernon Lee papers, Colby College, Maine, Manuscript Collections, letter 305.

16. Laurel Brake, 'Vernon Lee and the Pater Circle', Maxwell and Pulham, 40–57; Colby, 56–7, 62–4, 66–8; Stefano Evangelista, 'Vernon Lee and the Gender of Aestheticism', Maxwell and Pulham, 92–7, 104–9 and Zorn, xviii, 13, 54–9, 79.

17. Walter Pater, *The Renaissance: Studies in Art and Poetry* (Oxford, Oxford University Press: 1986), xxix, xxx, 153; emphasis mine. References to Pater hereafter in the text.

18. Richard Le Gallienne, *The Romantic 90s* (1926) (London: Putnam & Company, 1951), 94, 55. References to Le Gallienne hereafter in the text.

19. Patricia Pulham, *Art and the Transitional Object in Vernon Lee's Supernatural Tales* (Aldershot and Burlington VT: Ashgate, 2008), 130.

20. Jane Wood, *Passion and Pathology in Victorian Fiction* (Oxford: Oxford University Press, 2001), 163.

21. Richard Dellamora, *Masculine Desire, The Sexual Politics of Victorian Aestheticism*. Chapel Hill and London: University of North Carolina Press, 1990), 132, 146. Emphasis in original.

22. Ruth Robbins, 'Apparitions Can Be Deceptive, Vernon Lee's Androgynous Spectres' in *Victorian Gothic. Literary and Cultural Manifestations in the Nineteenth Century* (eds.) Ruth Robbins and Julian Wolfreys (Basingstoke: Palgrave, 2000), 186–8.

23. Frank Harris, *Oscar Wilde: His Life and Confessions* (New York: Horizon Press, 1974), 245.

24. Max Nordau, *Degeneration* (Lincoln, Nebraska & London: University of Nebraska Press, 1993), 1, 15, 288, 7.

25. Linda Dowling, 'The Decadent and the New Woman in the 1890's', *Nineteenth Century Fiction* 33:4 (March 1979), 447. References to Dowling hereafter in the text.

26. Contemporary reviews of *The Picture of Dorian Gray* were collected by Wilde's friend Stuart Mason in Oscar Wilde, *Art and Morality, A Defence of Dorian Gray* (ed.) Stuart Mason (London: F. Palmer, 1912).

27. *Speaker*, 13 April 1895, 403; see John Stokes, *In the Nineties* (Hemel Hempstead: Harvester Wheatsheaf, 1989), 14–15.

28. The *Daily Telegraph*, 27 May 1895, reprinted in Jonathan Goodman, *The Oscar Wilde File* (London: W. H. Allen & Co., 1988), 133; the *Evening News* quoted in Regenia Gagnier, *Idylls of the Marketplace: Oscar Wilde and the Victorian Public* (Aldershot: Scolar Press, 1987), 146.

29. Margaret D. Stetz 'The Snake Lady and the Bruised Bodley Head: Vernon Lee and Oscar Wilde in the *Yellow Book*', Maxwell and Pulham, 113–19.

30. Sally Ledger, *The New Woman: Fiction and Feminism at the Fin de Siècle* (Manchester and New York: Manchester University Press, 1997),

111–13.
31. Rev W. F. Barry, 'The Strike of A Sex' *Quarterly Review*, 179 (1894), 314.

CHAPTER 2. EXPERIMENTS IN SHORT FICTION

1. See Introduction, 3.
2. The region that Trepka hails from had been annexed by Prussia in 1793 and, according to Maxwell and Pulham, saw a major increase in German colonization in the nineteenth century, *HAOFT*, 42, n.1.
3. In an essay in *Euphorion*, 'The Italy of the Elizabethan Dramatists', Lee, unlike the fictional Trepka, refused to adopt a morally relativist attitude towards Lucrezia Borgia whom she roundly condemns for being 'passive to surrounding influences, blind to good and evil, infamous in the infamous Rome, among her father and brother's courtesans and cut-throats; grave and gracious in the grave and gracious Ferrara, among the Platonic poets and pacific courtiers of the court of the Estensi', *E*, 1:99.
4. The only fiction she published in this period were the short stories and novellas: *A Phantom Lover* (1886; reprinted as 'Oke of Okehurst', 1890), 'Amour Dure' (1887), 'A Wicked Voice' (1887) which along with 'Dionea' would appear in the collection *Hauntings* (1890), the collection *Vanitas: Polite Stories* (1892), the original French version of 'The Virgin of the Seven Daggers' ('La Madone aux sept glaives' (1896)) and the fairytale 'Prince Alberic and the Snake Lady' also published in 1896.
5. Henry James, preface to 'The Lesson of the Master', *The Art of the Novel, Critical Prefaces* (New York and London: Scribner's Sons, 1962), 219.
6. H. G. Wells, 'Introduction' to *The Country of the Blind and Other Stories* (London: Thomas Nelson & Sons, 1911), iv, vi.
7. Nigel Cross, *The Common Writer, Life in Nineteenth-Century Grub Street* (Cambridge: Cambridge University Press, 1985), 205.
8. George Gissing, *New Grub Street* (1891) (Harmondsworth: Penguin, 1985), 81.
9. Vineta Colby's description of Lee in *The Singular Anomaly: Women Novelists of the Nineteenth Century* (New York and London: New York University Press and London University Press, 1970), 235. Until 1482 this area of Spain had been populated and ruled by Muslims from North Africa (the Moors) after which time, a final war had brought the area back under Spanish and Christian rule. Muslims, 'Moriscos', were forced to convert to Christianity on pain of death.

10. In Marian discourse the seven swords represent the seven sorrows that Christ's Mother was said to have suffered.

11. Charles Baudelaire, 'À une Madone', *The Flowers of Evil (Les Fleurs du Mal)*, trans. James McGowan (Oxford: Oxford University Press, 1993), l.18, 119, and l.14, 1.16, 121.

12. Horace Walpole, *The Castle of Otranto* (Oxford: Oxford University Press, 1996), 5–9.

13. John Fowles, *The French Lieutenant's Woman* (1969) (Manchester: Triad Granada, 1977), 85–7.

14. In his review of Lee's anti-war play *Satan the Waster* (1920), George Bernard Shaw praised her as 'the old guard of Victorian cosmopolitan intellectualism' precisely because of this and her pacifist stance and 'salute[d] her as the noblest Briton of them all', quoted in Colby, 307.

CHAPTER 3. 'ART NOT FOR ART'S SAKE'

1. Lee's main predecessor in carrying out research into the psychology and physical effects of art-appreciation was Grant Allen in his *Physiological Aesthetics* (London: King, 1877), a text which Lee found reductive because she felt that it did not separate physiological processes from intellectual judgements. See *BU*, 172.

2. For example, in the *Daily Telegraph* Wilde and the Decadents were roundly castigated for their hieratic poses and what the *Daily Telegraph* ridiculed as their 'spasmodic search for ancient graces', *Daily Telegraph*, 6 April 1895, reprinted in Goodman, 75.

3. See Diana Maltz's account of these gallery tours in her essay 'Engaging "Delicate Brains": From Working- Class Enculturation to Upper-Class Lesbian Liberation in Vernon Lee and Kit Anstruther-Thomson's Psychological Aesthetics', in *Women and British Aestheticism* Talia Schaffer and Kathy Alexis Psomiades (eds.) (Charlottesville, VA and London: University Press of Virginia, 1999), 211–29. References to Maltz hereafter in the text.

4. C. Anstuther-Thomson, *Art and Man: Essays and Fragments, With Twenty Illustrations and an Introduction by Vernon Lee* (London: John Lane, 1924) 27. References to *AM* hereafter in the text.

5. Kathy Alexis Psomiades '"Still Burning from this Strangling Embrace": Vernon Lee on Desire and Aesthetics' in Richard Dellamora (ed.) *Victorian Sexual Dissidence*. (Chicago and London: The University of Chicago Press, 1999), 36.

6. Lee is referring to the Latin phrase 'vox clamans in deserto' here which translates as a 'lone voice crying in the wilderness'.

7. Vernon Lee, 'The Heart of a Neutral', *The Atlantic Monthly* CXVI

(November 1915), 687.

8. In her recollections of the Paget family, Mary Robinson describes Lee's mother as a resident of 'Cosmopolis', a description which could be equally applied to Lee, quoted in Gunn, 19.

9. Hilary Fraser, 'Evelyn De Morgan, Vernon Lee, and Assimilation from Without', *Journal of Pre-Raphaelite Studies*, NS 14 (Spring, 2005), 88.

10. Colby wrongly accredits this idea to David Seed in his 'Introduction' to Vernon Lee, *The Handling of Words and Other Studies in Literary Psychology* (Lampeter: Edwin Mellen, 1992), i–xxx.

11. Christa Zorn, '*The Handling of Words*: Reader Response Victorian Style' in Maxwell and Pulham, 176.

12. Lee writes 'I cannot assert these things as certain, but only suspect them; and I pass alongside of that Dionysiac art, in lack of understanding, but in awe and humility', *HW*, 114.

Select Bibliography

WORKS BY VERNON LEE

Tuscan Fairy Tales, Taken Down from the Mouths of the People. London: W. Satchell, 1880. Published anonymously.

Studies of the Eighteenth Century in Italy. London: W. Satchell, 1880.

Belcaro: Being Essays on Sundry Æsthetical Questions. London: W. Satchell, 1881.

Ottilie: an Eighteenth-Century Idyl. London: T. Fisher Unwin, 1883.

The Prince of a Hundred Soups: A Puppet-Show in Narrative. London: T. Fisher Unwin, 1883.

Euphorion: Being Studies of the Antique and the Mediæval in the Renaissance. 2 vols. London: T. Fisher Unwin, 1884.

The Countess of Albany. Eminent Women Series. London: W. H. Allen, 1884.

Miss Brown: A Novel. 3 vols. Edinburgh and London: William Blackwood and Sons, 1884.

A Phantom Lover: A Fantastic Story. Edinburgh and London: William Blackwood and Sons, 1886. Reprinted as 'Oke of Okehurst; Or, the Phantom Lover' in *Hauntings: Fantastic Stories*.

Baldwin: Being Dialogues on Views and Aspirations. London: T. Fisher Unwin, 1886.

Juvenilia: Essays on Sundry Æsthetical Questions. 2 vols. London: T. Fisher Unwin, 1887.

Hauntings: Fantastic Stories. London: Heinemann, 1890. Bodley Head, 1906. Features the novellas 'Amour Dure', 'Dionea', 'Oke of Okehurst; or, A Phantom Lover' and 'A Wicked Voice'.

Vanitas: Polite Stories. London: W. Heinemann, 1892. Features the novellas 'Lady Tal', 'A Worldly Woman' and 'The Legend of Madame Krasinska'.

Althea: A Second Book of Dialogues on Aspirations and Duties. London: Osgood, McIlvaine, 1894.

Renaissance Fancies and Studies: A Sequel to Euphorion. London: Smith, Elder & Co., 1895.

Limbo and Other Essays. London: Grant Richards, 1897.

Genius Loci: Notes on Places. London: Grant Richards, 1899.

Penelope Brandling: A Tale of the Welsh Coast in the Eighteenth Century. London: T. Fisher Unwin, 1903.

Ariadne in Mantua: A Romance in Five Acts. Oxford: Basil Blackwell, 1903.

Pope Jacynth and Other Fantastic Tales. London: Grant Richards, 1904.

Hortus Vitae: Essays on the Gardening of Life. London: John Lane, The Bodley Head, 1904.

The Enchanted Woods and Other Essays. London: John Lane, The Bodley Head, 1905.

The Spirit of Rome: Leaves from a Diary. London: John Lane, The Bodley Head, 1906.

Sister Benvenuta and the Christ Child: an Eighteenth-Century Legend. London: Grant Richards, 1906.

The Sentimental Traveller: Notes on Places. London: John Lane, The Bodley Head, 1908.

Gospels of Anarchy and Other Contemporary Studies. London: T. Fisher Unwin, 1908. Includes 'The Deterioration of the Soul' Lee's 1897 essay against Max Nordau's *Degeneration* and 'The Economic Parasitism of Women' (1902), Lee's review essay of Charlotte Perkins Gilman's *Women and Economics* (1898).

Limbo and Other Essays, to Which is Now Added Ariadne in Mantua. London: John Lane, The Bodley Head, 1908.

Laurus Nobilis: Chapters on Art and Life. London: John Lane, The Bodley Head, 1909.

Vital Lies: Studies of Some Varieties of Recent Obscurantism. London: John Lane, The Bodley Head, 1912.

Beauty and Ugliness, with Clementina Anstruther-Thomson. London: John Lane, The Bodley Head, 1912.

The Beautiful; An Introduction to Psychological Aesthetics. Cambridge Manuals of Science and Literature, 77. Cambridge: Cambridge University Press, 1913.

The Tower of the Mirrors and Other Essays on the Spirit of Places. London: John Lane, The Bodley Head, 1914.

Louis Norbert: A Two-Fold Romance. London: John Lane, The Bodley Head, 1914.

The Ballet of the Nations: a Present-Day Morality. London: Chatto & Windus, 1915.

Peace with Honour: Controversial Notes on the Settlement. London: Union of Democratic Control, 1915.

Satan the Waster: a Philosophic War Trilogy with Notes and Introduction. London: John Lane, The Bodley Head, 1920.

The Handling of Words and Other Studies in Literary Psychology. London: John Lane, The Bodley Head, 1923.

Art and Man, Essays and Fragments, by Clementina Anstruther-Thomson,

Lee, Vernon (ed.) Introduction by Vernon Lee. London: John Lane, The Bodley Head, 1924.

The Golden Keys and Other Essays on the Genius Loci. London: John Lane, The Bodley Head, 1925.

Proteus: Or, the Future of Intelligence. London: Kegan Paul, 1925.

The Poet's Eye: Notes on Some Difference between Verse and Prose. London: Hogarth Press, 1926.

For Maurice: Five Unlikely Stories. London: John Lane, The Bodley Head, 1927.

Music and Its Lovers: An Empirical Study of Emotional and Imaginative Responses to Music, with Clementina Anstruther-Thomson. London: G. Allen & Unwin, 1932.

Supernatural Tales: Excursions into Fantasy. London: Peter Owen, 1955.

Pope Jacynth, and More Supernatural Tales. London: Peter Owen, 1956.

Hauntings and Other Fantastic Tales, (eds.) Catherine Maxwell and Patricia Pulham (Peterborough, Canada: Broadview Press, 2006). An indispensable edition of Lee's supernatural tales, meticulously edited with an excellent introduction and useful appendices. Features 'Amour Dure', 'Dionea', 'Oke of Okehurst', 'A Wicked Voice', 'Prince Alberic and the Snake Lady', 'A Wedding Chest' and 'The Virgin of the Seven Daggers'.

CRITICAL AND BIOGRAPHICAL WORKS ON VERNON LEE

Beer, Gillian, 'The Dissidence of Vernon Lee: *Satan the Waster* and *The Will to Believe*', in Suzanne Raitt and Trudi Tate (eds.), *Women's Fiction and the Great War.* Oxford: Clarendon Press, 1997. 107–31. A pioneering reading of *Satan the Waster.*

Caballero, Carlo, ' "A Wicked Voice": on Vernon Lee, Wagner, and the Effects of Music', *Victorian Studies,* 35: 4 (Summer 1992): 385–408.

Colby, Vineta 'The Puritan Aesthete: Vernon Lee' in *The Singular Anomaly: Women Novelists of the Nineteenth Century.* New York and London: New York University Press and London University Press, 1970. 235–304.

_____, *Vernon Lee: A Literary Biography.* Charlottesville and London: University of Virginia Press, 2003. An intelligent and sympathetic biography.

Dellamora, Richard, 'Productive Decadence: "The Queer Comradeship of Outlawed Thought": Vernon Lee, Max Nordau, and Oscar Wilde'. *New Literary History* 35 (2005): 1–18. An interesting triangulation of Lee, Nordau and Wilde.

Denisoff, Dennis, 'The Forest Beyond the Frame: Picturing Women's Desires in Vernon Lee and Virginia Woolf' in Talia Schaffer and

Kathy Alexis Psomiades (eds.), *Women and British Aestheticism*. Charlottesville, VA: University of Virginia, 2000. 251–69. A suggestive reading of 'Oke of Okehurst'.

Fraser, Hilary, 'Women and the Ends of Art History: Vision and Corporeality in Nineteenth Century Discourse', *Victorian Studies* 42: 1 (1988–89), 77–100. An intelligent article which places *Miss Brown* and the psychological aesthetics project in relation to contemporary art-history.

_____, 'Interstitial Identities: Vernon Lee and the Spaces In-Between' in Demoor, Marysa (ed.), *Marketing the Author: Authorial Personae, Narrative Selves and Self-Fashioning, 1880–1930*. Houndmills, Basingstoke and New York: Palgrave Macmillan, 2004. 114–133. A persuasive postcolonial reading of Lee's expatriate national identity.

_____, 'Vernon Lee, England, Italy and Identity Politics', in Carol Richardson and Graham Smith (eds.), *Britannia Italia Germania: Taste and Travel in the Nineteenth Century*. Edinburgh: University of Edinburgh Press, 2001. 175–91.

Gunn, Peter, *Vernon Lee, Violet Paget, 1856–1935*. London: Oxford University Press, 1964. The first biography of Lee.

Leighton, Angela, 'Resurrections of the Body: Women Writers and the Idea of the Renaissance', in Alison Chapman and Jane Stabler (eds.), *Unfolding the South: Nineteenth Century British Women Writers and Artists in Italy 1789–1900*. Manchester: Manchester University Press, 2003. 222–38. A powerful reading of Lee's response to Italian culture.

Maltz, Diana, 'Engaging "Delicate Brains". From Working–Class Enculturation to Upper-Class Lesbian Liberation in Vernon Lee and Kit Anstruther-Thomson's *Psychological Aesthetics*', in Talia Schaffer and Kathy Alexis Psomiades (eds.), *Women and British Aestheticism*, Charlottesville, VA and London: University Press of Virginia, 1999. 211–29. A lively reading of the psychological aesthetics project.

Mannocchi, Phyllis F., 'Vernon Lee and Kit Anstruther–Thomson: a Study of Love and Collaboration Between Romantic Friends', *Women's Studies* 12 (1986): 129–48.

Maxwell, Catherine, 'Vernon Lee and the Ghosts of Italy' in Alison Chapman and Jane Stabler (eds.), *Unfolding the South: Nineteenth Century British Women Writers and Artists in Italy 1700–1900*. Manchester: Manchester University Press, 2003. 201–21.

_____ and Patricia Pulham (eds). *Vernon Lee: Decadence, Ethics, Aesthetics*. Basingstoke & New York: Palgrave Macmillan, 2006. A groundbreaking collection of essays re-evaluating Lee's work. Includes chapters by Laurel Brake, Grace Brockington, Stefano

Evangelista, Margaret Stetz and Christa Zorn.

Ormond, Leonée, 'Vernon Lee as a Critic of Aestheticism in *Miss Brown'*. *Colby Literary Quaterly* 9: 3 (1970): 131–54. Contains some interesting material on Lee's first visit to London.

Plain, Gill, 'The Shape of Things to Come: the Remarkable Modernity of Vernon Lee's *Satan the Waster* (1915–1920)', in Claire Tylee (ed.), *Women, the First World War and the Dramatic Imagination. International Essays (1914–1919)*. Lewiston, New York and Lampeter: Edwin Mellen Press, 2000, 5–21.

Psomiades, Kathy Alexis, ' "Still Burning from this Strangling Embrace": Vernon Lee on Desire and Aesthetics', in Richard Dellamora (ed.), *Victorian Sexual Dissidence*. Chicago and London: The University of Chicago Press, 1999: 21–41. A highly persuasive reading of the links between *Miss Brown* and the psychological aesthetics project.

Pulham, Patricia, *Art and the Transitional Object in Vernon Lee's Supernatural Tales*. Aldershot and Burlington VT: Ashgate, 2008. A fascinating psychoanalytical reading of Lee's supernatural fiction.

Robbins, Ruth, 'Apparitions Can Be Deceptive, Vernon Lee's Androgynous Spectres', in Ruth Robbins and Julian Wolfreys (eds.), *Victorian Gothic. Literary and Cultural Manifestations in the Nineteenth Century*. Basingstoke: Palgrave, 2000. 182–200.

Towheed, Shafquat, 'Determining "Fluctuating Opinions": Vernon Lee, Popular Fiction, and Theories of Reading', *Nineteenth-Century Literature*, 60:2 (September 2005), 199–236.

Vicinus, Martha, 'The Adolescent Boy: Fin de Siècle Femme Fatale?' *Journal of the History of Homosexuality* 5 (1994), 90–114. Reads 'Prince Alberic and the Snake Lady' as a lesbian text.

Zorn, Christa, 'Aesthetic Intertextuality as Cultural Critique: Vernon Lee Rewrites History Through Walter Pater's "La Gioconda" '. *The Victorian Newsletter* 91 (Spring 1997), 4–11. An intelligent reading of 'Amour Dure'.

_____, *Vernon Lee: Aesthetics, History and the Victorian Female Intellectual*. Ohio: Ohio University Press, 2003. A highly insightful analysis of Lee's work of the Victorian period, particularly with regards to the questions of gender and the emergent field of cultural history.

Index

Lightning Source UK Ltd.
Milton Keynes UK
03 February 2011

166888UK00001B/13/P